1986

The Art of Abstracting

Cover illustration: "Equinox" by Aldolph Gottlieb (1963), oil on canvas, 90 x 84 inches, unsigned.

—The Phillips Collection, Washington

The Professional Writing Series

This volume is one of a series published by ISI Press®. The series is designed to improve the communication skills of professional men and women, as well as students embarking upon professional careers.

Books published, in press, or in preparation for this series:

Communication Skills for the Foreign-Born Professional
     by GREGORY A. BARNES

The Art of Abstracting
     by EDWARD T. CREMMINS

How to Write and Publish a Scientific Paper
     by ROBERT A. DAY

How to Write and Publish Papers in the Medical Sciences
     by EDWARD J. HUTH

How to Write and Publish Engineering Papers and Reports
     by HERBERT B. MICHAELSON

The Art of Abstracting

EDWARD T. CREMMINS

iSi PRESS™

PHILADELPHIA

Published by

ⁱSⁱ PRESS® A Subsidiary of the
Institute for Scientific Information®
3501 Market St., University City Science Center, Philadelphia, PA 19104 U.S.A.

© 1982 ISI Press

ISBN 0-89495-015-0

Library of Congress Cataloging in Publication Data

Cremmins, Edward T. 1929–
  The art of abstracting.

  (The Professional writing series)
  Bibliography: p.
  Includes index.
  1. Abstracting. 2. Abstracting and indexing services. 3. English language—Technical
English. 4. English language—Business English. I. Title. II. Series.
PE1477.C7 1982   808'.062   82-9272
ISBN 0-89495-015-0 (pbk.)   AACR2

Printed in the United States of America

ABSTRACT:

A three-stage analytical reading method is described for the writing of informative and indicative abstracts by authors and abstracting-service (access) abstractors. Good reading, thinking, writing, and editing skills are required for good abstracting. Adherence to rules and conventions for abstracting and the maintenance of cooperative professional relationships also contribute to the preparation of high-quality abstracts.

Preface

*Writing is one art form that can be practiced almost
anywhere at almost any time. Normally, you cannot paint
in the office, or sculpture in the classroom, or play the
piano in a plane or the trumpet on a train. But, given
some paper and a writing implement, one can write in any
of these places. What emerges will not always be a work
of art; yet it could be. At the very least we can introduce
clarity, precision, and grace into the most ordinary of our
written communications.*
— THEODORE M. BERNSTEIN[6]

I feel certain that the late Theodore Bernstein, who was a distinguished assistant managing editor of *The New York Times* and a faculty member of Columbia's School of Journalism, would have included abstracting among the subforms of writing. While practicing the art of abstracting for almost 15 years, I have indeed written abstracts almost anywhere at almost any time. Occasionally, the writing has been done as a passenger on commuter buses and trains, but more often it has been done in the offices of information-service facilities. If a panel of my fellow abstractors were formed, it might even judge a few abstracts among the thousands that I have written to be minor works of the abstractor's art. If this were to happen, it would primarily be the result of my efforts to introduce into the abstracts those qualities of clarity, precision, and grace cited by Bernstein, in combination with the greatest possible amount of information within the constraints of time and the specified length of the abstract.

The purpose of this book is to assist authors of scientific and scholarly works and abstractors for abstract journals and information systems in writing abstracts that attempt to meet Bernstein's criteria for consideration as works of art. The book is also intended for use as a textbook on abstracting within library and information-science departments of universities and colleges.

The book is not intended to supplant the excellent general guidebooks and articles on abstracting already in print, nor the many fine style manuals used by abstracting services. Rather, the aim is to complement them by presenting practical advice on the reading, thinking, writing, and editing tasks that comprise the abstracting process.

In the 14 years since I wrote my first abstract, I have worked on a broad range of information systems as an abstractor, indexer, editor, trainer of other abstractors, translator, and lexicographer. Four of the 14 years were spent at the National Aeronautics and Space Administration (NASA) Scientific and Technical Information Facility. The other 10 years included assignments as managing editor of *Cancer Chemotherapy Abstracts* (now *Cancer Therapy Abstracts*) and *EIS: Key to Environmental Impact Statements* (now *EIS: Digests of Environmental Impact Statements*) and as assistant managing editor of *Mental Retardation Abstracts* (since ceased publication).

While editing the thousands of abstracts of the many abstractors with whom I have had direct contact over the years and those written by authors with whom I have had no contact whatsoever, I have become convinced that far too many informative abstracts from both authors and abstractors fail to inform adequately and that a proportionately equal fraction of indicative or descriptive abstracts from the same sources either indicate or describe too much or too little information. If this book makes a contribution toward alleviating this problem, its primary purpose will have been fulfilled.

One of the themes of this book holds that the development and maintenance of cooperative professional relationships between abstractors, editors, managers, sponsors of abstracting services, and users of abstracts are vital to the composition of well-construed abstracts. Similar cooperative relationships have been vital to the composition of this book. I am deeply indebted to Ben Weil (rhymes with *style*), who reviewed two versions of the manuscript and offered numerous suggestions on how to make it less indicative and more informative and instructive.

Other debts of gratitude I hasten to acknowledge are to three colleagues who reviewed a draft version of the manuscript: Bevin Grylack, Linda Sexton, and Nancy Wright (who also steadfastly furnished worthwhile advice on the effective management of the research and writing and the drafting of correspondence related to the manuscript).

I would like to express my appreciation to many of my present co-workers at Tracor (JITCO). Marji Trachtman has been an inspirational model as she progressed rapidly through the assignments of abstractor-in-training, proficient abstractor, editor, and manager and trainer of abstractors. Other co-workers who contributed generously of their management, technical, or information-processing expertise include Bill Theriault, Randy Huffman, Hal Halpin, Esther Asaki, Tim Morrison, Nancy Adams, Linda Suit, Marjorie Roher, Karen Bowman, Dottie Beauregard, Lois Blaine, Reva Fox, Ginny Shreve, Mark Pielmeier, and Rita Mazzitti. The

Chinese-American artist Diana Lin shared pertinent thoughts on the art of abstract painting.

Other colleagues from the fields of information science and scholarly publishing who made worthwhile suggestions during the preparation of the book are Edmond Sawyer, Karl Heumann, Mark Carroll, Elizabeth Fake, Barbara Meyers, Josh Smith, Emil Levine, Toni Carbo Bearman, Gene Allen, David Batty, Madeline Henderson, Samuel Beatty, Lynn Barnett, and Pat Foreman.

William Wilson and Ruth Zeender furnished guidance and full access to research materials in the collection of the College of Library and Information Services at the University of Maryland.

Finally, I thank Estella Bradley, my manuscript editor at ISI Press, for furnishing me with the necessary finishing touches in the process of my transition from access abstractor to author.

Cooperative familial relationships were also indispensable. In appreciation, I dedicate this book to my wife Jo-Ann and to Edward, Julie, and Danny.

Contents

PART I

ABSTRACTS AND ABSTRACTING

INDICATIVE ABSTRACT:

The functional and creative writing characteristics of abstracting are discussed. The types of published materials that are abstracted are described, and the value of abstracts to readers, authors, professional abstractors, primary publishers and editors, and information specialists is mentioned. The content and types of abstracts are also described. The processes of human and computer-assisted abstracting and translating are compared.

1

Chapter 1

About Abstracting

What Is an Abstract?

Within the literature on information science, scholarly publishing, and technical writing, answers to the question "What is an abstract?" are as varied in length and content as the actual abstracts that are published in different abstract journals. The American National Standards Institute's definition is one of the most terse: "An abstract is defined as an abbreviated, accurate representation of the contents of a document, preferably prepared by its author(s) for publication with it. Such abstracts are also useful in access publications and machine-readable data bases."[2]

Good abstracts are highly structured, concise, and coherent, and are the result of a thorough analysis of the content of the abstracted materials. Abstracts may be more readable than the basic documents, but because of size constraints they rarely equal and never surpass the information content of the basic document.

Well-written abstracts have been described by Ashworth as the product of the highest craftsmanship:

> To take an original article, understand it and pack it neatly into a nutshell without loss of substance or clarity presents a challenge which many have felt worth taking up for the joys of achievement alone. These are the characteristics of an art form.[4]

The art of abstracting demands the application of extensive reading, thinking, writing, and editing skills. In Parts II through IV of this text, this fact is discussed in detail. The remainder of Part I presents additional background information on the abstracting process.

What Is Abstracted?

Primary publishers furnish abstracts with almost all of the articles on theoretical or experimental research that they publish. These publishers

3

normally do not provide abstracts with editorial material, short communications, or letters to the editor. "Access" (abstracting and indexing) publishers either publish collections of abstracts in abstract journals or maintain them in files that now are generally stored in computer memories for retrieval on demand. In addition to comprehensive coverage of the items that are abstracted in relevant primary publications, access publishers also selectively abstract books, editorials, patents, research progress reports, conference proceedings, and letters to the editors of scholarly publications that contain substantive information of lasting value. Other access publishers abstract the information contained in such nonprint materials as filmstrips, cassette tapes, and visual aids.

Value of Abstracts

Abstracts assist readers in deciding whether they should consult the full text of the material that is abstracted because it contains information that will satisfy their needs.

Besides their primary value to readers of scholarly and technical monographs and journals, abstracts are of importance to authors, professional abstractors, primary publishers, editors, and information specialists. When authors of research papers and monographs write their own abstracts, they are given an additional opportunity to evaluate the style and content of their writing and to identify and correct shortcomings.

Professionals who abstract documents that have been published without an abstract or who revise author-written abstracts to conform to the specifications of alerting or information-retrieval systems can earn substantial income if they are proficient and highly productive. Subject specialists or volunteer abstractors who write abstracts as an avocation are aided in keeping abreast of advances in their fields of interest.

Author abstracts that accompany manuscripts submitted for publication ease the selection process for the editorial staffs of primary publishers. Staff editors can use the abstracts to estimate the depth of treatment and degree of originality of such material. The information in the abstract may even indicate portions of the text that need to be expanded, clarified, or eliminated. Author abstracts also can be used as a primary source of ideas for promoting the contents of the journals or conference proceedings in which they are published.

Information specialists who depend on abstracts to assist them in their work include indexers, information-retrieval analysts, and lexicographers.

Types of Abstracts

Abstracts often are classified on the basis of content, purpose, and structure as well as their authorship. Abstracts of articles in primary journals are usually called *author abstracts*, although some are written by subject specialists or members of the editorial staff of the publishing house. Abstracts written for secondary publications and services typically are composed by subject or information specialists. Since these secondary publications and services have now become better known as access publications and services, the abstracts prepared for them will be referred to as *access abstracts* in this text.

Author and access abstracts may be further classified according to purpose, structure, content, and method of preparation. Within this classification scheme, the two most common types are *informative* and *indicative* abstracts, which will be discussed shortly. Other types include *modular*, *critical*, and *computer-based* abstracts. All of these abstract types are described in the Glossary at the end of this book.

Content of Abstracts

Abstracts generally contain up to four, usually sequential, information elements that describe or extract information from the basic document. As described in the *American National Standard for Writing Abstracts*, these elements state the "purpose, methodology, results, and conclusions presented in the original document."[2] Methods for preparing this type of abstract are those that generally will be discussed in this book. A *findings-oriented* abstract, in which the most important results or conclusions are placed first, followed by supporting details, other findings, and methodology, is also mentioned in the *American National Standard for Writing Abstracts*. Once authors or access abstractors acquire a good understanding of the procedures for writing the more conventional types of abstracts, they should have no difficulty in writing findings-oriented abstracts or other types that use variations in format. When examples of abstracts are discussed in the following pages of this book, the four information elements are referred to by slightly different terms. These are (1) primary annotative element (information on purpose, scope, and methodology comprising the first sentence); (2) secondary annotative element (those sentences, if any, containing additional information on purpose, scope, and methodology); (3) results; and (4) conclusions and recommendations.

Indicative and Informative Abstracts

Indicative and informative abstracts are variously defined in the literature. Many definitions suggest that an informative abstract should be a miniature version of the full paper, whereas an indicative abstract should resemble a table of contents. In practice, the differences between the two types often become blurred. The *American National Standard* accordingly recognizes the existence of mixed "informative–indicative" abstracts.

For ease of instruction in this text, I consider indicative abstracts to be those which contain information on the purpose, scope, or methodology, but not on results, conclusions, or recommendations. An example of this type of abstract is given in Figure 1. Each of the five parts of this book is introduced with an indicative abstract.

The preferred definition for an informative abstract in this text is that, although it may contain information on purpose, scope, and methods, it must also contain results, conclusions, or recommendations. Figure 2 shows an informative abstract that contains all four information elements. In Figure 3, the indicative abstract given in Figure 1 has been expanded into an informative abstract by the addition of a conclusion.

Progress in modeling human cognitive processes is reviewed, emphasizing the use of computer programming languages as a formalism for modeling and computer simulation of the behavior of the systems modeled. Elementary and higher processes are examined, and neural models are briefly described.

FIG. 1. *Indicative abstract. Adapted from the abstract in Simon.*[27]

The embryotoxicity of hexachlorocyclopentadiene was studied in mice and rabbits. Pregnant animals were given 5, 25, or 75 mg/kg per day by gavage on days 6 to 15 (mice) or days 6 to 18 (rabbits) of gestation. Food and water consumption and weight were recorded daily. Mice and rabbit dams were killed on days 18 and 29 of gestation, respectively. Fetuses were removed and examined for malformations. Fertility of the treated mice and rabbits was not significantly different from that of control animals. The dose of 75 mg/kg per day was toxic to rabbit dams; no toxic effects were seen in mice at any dose. No significant effects on the average number of implantations, live fetuses, or resorptions were observed in either species.

FIG. 2. *Informative abstract. Not published previously.*

Progress in modeling human cognitive processes is reviewed, emphasizing the use of computer programming languages as a formalism for modeling and computer simulation of the behavior of the systems modeled. Elementary and higher processes are examined, and neural models are briefly described. Theories of human cognitive processes can be attempted at the levels of neural, elementary information (retrieval from memory, scanning down lists in memory, comparing simple symbols), or higher information processes (problem solving, concept attainment).

FIG. 3. *Informative version of the Figure 1 indicative abstract.*

Chapter 2

Informative Words
for Authors of Abstracts

> *There are four things that make this world go round:*
> *love, energy, materials, and information. We see about us*
> *a critical shortage of the first commodity, a near-critical*
> *shortage of the second, increasing shortage of the third,*
> *but an absolute glut of the fourth.*
> —ROBERT A. DAY

In the preface to his book *How to Write and Publish a Scientific Paper*,[12] Day uses the four words love, energy, materials, and information to underscore his general advice to authors of scientific papers before he presents more specific advice, not only on the writing of a scientific paper but also on writing review papers, conference reports, and theses. Continuing his preface, Day advises authors on how to alleviate the problem of the glut of information:

> We in science, of necessity, must contribute to the glut. But let us do it with love, especially love of the English language, which is the cornerstone of our intellectual heritage; let us do it with energy, the energy we need to put into the scientific paper so that the reader will not need to use much energy to get the information out of the paper; and let us husband our materials, especially our words, so that we do not waste inordinate quantities of paper and ink in trying to tell the world more than we know.

That which is appropriate for the writing of all other components of a scientific or scholarly paper is also appropriate for the writing of the abstract.

Second-Wind Love and Energy

Everyone knows what it is to start a piece of work, either intellectual or muscular, feeling stale—or *oold*, as an Adirondack guide once put

7

it to me. And everybody knows what it is to "warm up" to his job. The process of warming up gets particularly striking in the phenomenon known as "second wind."

—WILLIAM JAMES

The original or revised version of the author's paper is almost completed. He (or she) has invested far more love, energy, and time in thinking through his ideas, researching them, testing them, and writing them into manuscript form than he ever imagined he would when he first decided to share them through publication. The paper now has unity and coherence, and the ideas flow well from the introduction to the conclusions and recommendations; footnotes are numbered and verified, and are in proper sequence; and references are in agreement with the specifications of the publisher to whom the manuscript is being submitted. One of the final steps remaining before submission of the full manuscript for refereeing, review, or acceptance is to prepare or revise the abstract.

This seems simple enough. Besides a few minor "style conventions" on verb usage, symbols, and abbreviations, the instructions for the particular abstract might ask only for an "informative abstract" of about 150 words. This appears to pose no major problem, even though the author now may be feeling intellectually "stale—or *oold*," as William James put it in his 1906 essay on "The Energies of Men."[15] But if he or she does not have a firm grasp of the fundamentals of preparing an informative abstract, this request definitely could pose a major problem—one which could well require a substantial burst of "second-wind" love and energy to ensure that the completed abstract achieves the same degree of unity as the full text of the paper that follows it.

Information Reductionism

Science gets most of its information by the process of reductionism, exploring the details, then the details of the details, until all the smallest bits of the structure, or the smallest parts of the mechanism, are laid out for counting and scrutiny.

The above definition of the scientific process created by Lewis Thomas,[29] a contemporary essayist and biology watcher, may be paraphrased to define the abstracting process:

Abstracts derive most of their substantive information by a process of reductionism, the analytical reading of the full text of a paper, monograph, or thesis, until all of the relevant parts of the structure and the essence of the findings and conclusions are laid out for writing and editing.

Primary authors should consider the process of writing abstracts to be an all-out effort in information reductionism or condensation, no matter what style, content, or form is required for the abstract. Reductionism also should be the primary consideration, no matter what type of written, spoken, or visual material is being abstracted, whether it be a monograph, a description of a scientific method, a statement of plans or policies, a review of the literature, an epidemiological survey, a mathematical analysis, an experimental study using materials, animals, or humans, a conference proceedings, a hearing transcript, or a personal-opinion paper based on practical experience or theoretical speculation.

Finally, authors should be unrelenting information reductionists throughout the full abstract-preparation cycle of reading, thinking, writing, and editing, whether these skills are used concurrently or sequentially. Throughout this preparation cycle, William Strunk's terse advice to "omit needless words" to achieve conciseness therefore might be expanded as follows and applied unremittingly: omit needless paragraphs, sentences, and words and phrases within sentences.

Materials Handling

6. DO NOT ERASE. Remember that your abstract will appear in Federation Proceedings exactly as you submit it; any erasure, smudges, errors, misspellings, poor hyphenations and deviations from good usage will be glaringly apparent in the published abstract.

The above statement is from the instructions for the submission of abstracts for the meetings convened by the Federation of American Societies for Experimental Biology (FASEB). These instructions are extremely detailed, because the large number of these abstracts and the rigid meeting deadlines necessitate that abstracts be submitted in the form of "camera-ready copy." Consequently, these abstracts receive a minimum of editorial processing before they are printed in the journal *Federation Proceedings* and distributed at the FASEB meetings.

Although abstracts submitted to most other primary publishers are given a greater amount of pre-publication editorial processing than the FASEB meeting abstracts, authors should, nevertheless, prepare their abstracts with the same high degree of care throughout the process as they would if the abstracts were, in fact, scheduled for treatment as camera-ready copy.

When the publisher furnishes a set of instructions on abstract preparation, the author should read them carefully and comply with them strictly. In accordance with the design specifications for the full publication, the publisher determines the precise form of the abstracts that will appear in the publication. The readers of a particular publication become accustomed to the style in which the abstracts are presented; therefore, unconventional forms should not be used. If, however, as an author you are convinced that the publisher's instructions hinder the writing of concise, informative abstracts, follow them as completely as possible, but enclose separate, well-documented suggestions for improving the instructions along with your abstract.

A few general suggestions for preparing standard abstracts follow. The suggestions are based on practical experience, the FASEB instructions, and guidelines contained in the *American National Standard for Writing Abstracts.*

- Prepare an abstract that access services can reproduce with little or no change, copyright permitting.
- State the purpose, methods, results, and conclusions presented in the original document, either in that order or with initial emphasis on results and conclusions.
- Make the abstract as informative as the nature of the document will permit, so that readers may decide, quickly and accurately, whether they need to read the entire document.
- Unless otherwise instructed, use fewer than 250 words for most papers and portions of monographs and fewer than 100 words for notes and short communications. For long reports and theses, do not exceed 500 words.
- Avoid including background information or citing the work of others in the abstract, unless the study is a replication or evaluation of their work.
- Do not include information in the abstract that is not contained in the textual material being abstracted.
- Verify that all quantitative or qualitative information used in the abstract agrees with the information contained in the full text of the document.
- Use standard English and precise technical terms, and follow conventional grammar and punctuation rules.
- Give expanded versions of lesser known abbreviations and acronyms, and verbalize symbols that may be unfamiliar to readers of the abstract.
- Omit needless words, phrases, and sentences.

Chapter 3

Abstracting and Translating: Man–Machine Copywriting?

```
MAN–MACHINE SYSTEMS
    RT  ASTRONAUT PERFORMANCE
        AUTOMATION
        BALANCING
        BIOTICS
        BIOTECHNOLOGY
        CONSOLES
        DATA-PROCESSING TERMINALS
        DEPERSONALIZATION
        DISPLAY DEVICES
        ENGINEERING
        HUMAN-FACTORS ENGINEERING
        MECHANIZATION
        SYSTEMS ANALYSIS
        SYSTEMS ENGINEERING
```

As one might infer from the first "related term" (RT) listed (ASTRO-NAUT PERFORMANCE), the indexing term MAN–MACHINE SYSTEMS is contained in the indexing and retrieval thesaurus for the NASA scientific and technical information system. To characterize the following brief discussion on human and machine- or computer-assisted abstracting and translating, I will construct a new indexing term: MAN–MACHINE COPYWRITING, using part of the primary heading and some of the related terms for the NASA term MAN–MACHINE SYSTEMS.

```
MAN–MACHINE COPYWRITING
    RT  ABSTRACTING
        ALGORITHMS
        ARTIFICIAL INTELLIGENCE
        COGNITIVE SCIENCE
        COMPUTATIONAL LINGUISTICS
        COPYING
```

11

CYBERNETICS
EXTRACTING
HUMAN-FACTORS ENGINEERING
SYSTEMS ENGINEERING
TRANSLATING

Abstracting and Translating as Copying Functions

Aren't abstracting and translating for the most part equivalent to copying functions? Both functions do involve extensive copying or extracting of the content of textual information. Both writing activities now are performed by both man and machines. Man has been writing abstracts since at least the eighteenth century and began writing translations long before that time. Serious attempts at perfecting machine translating and then machine abstracting were begun shortly after World War II. The computer is programmed to perform word lookup and semantic or statistical analyses of textual materials, or to use techniques of human intelligence simulation to devise formalisms for replacing or assisting translators or abstractors in the copying process.

But are translating and abstracting, in fact, primarily only exercises in copying or extracting information? By no means! Indeed, I am certain that most information- and computer-science researchers, practitioners, and managers would strongly dispute the validity of my glib indexing term MAN–MACHINE COPYWRITING and might suggest that the results of abstracting or translating done with this simplistic notion in mind would more closely resemble artificial extracts and transliterations than true abstracts and translations, respectively.

Since it is beyond the instructional scope of this book, no further discussion of translating will be presented. Although the primary emphasis of the discussion will continue to be on human abstracting techniques, appropriate comparative references will be made to the subject of machine- or computer-assisted abstracting.

Human and computer-assisted abstracting does, of necessity, involve a certain amount of copying or extracting, but it is a much more complex procedure than this would imply. The complexity of computer-assisted abstracting is evident in the fact that, of the eight different machine approaches involving statistical and linguistic techniques cited by Mathis in 1972,[22] only one had advanced even barely beyond the experimental stage. Since that time, the literature on experimental or operational automatic abstracting systems has been sparse. Recent intensified interest in the application of cognitive science, computational linguistics, and artificial intelligence techniques to information processing, however, should stimulate still further attempts to advance computer-assisted abstracting.

The fact that human abstracting is more complex than just copying or extracting becomes clear from the findings of studies on the quality of abstracts and on inter-abstractor consistency, and particularly from Borko and Chatman's survey of sets of instructions for abstractors,[9] the series of articles on abstracting by Weil et al.,[33,34,35] and the specifications in the *American National Standard for Writing Abstracts.*[2] Abstractors must have a good grasp of and be able to apply the principles of analytical reading, logical thinking, informative writing, and concise editing. Accordingly, the remaining materials in the first four parts of this book in their broadest context might be indexed with the following single term:

INFORMATIVE ABSTRACTING
RT   ANALYTICAL READING
      CONCISE EDITING
      COPYING
      EXTRACTING
      INFORMATIVE WRITING
      LOGICAL THINKING

Chapter 4

Information Selection
and Relevance for Abstracts

*Programming the computer to select "significant
representative sentences" required precise operational
instructions, and this in turn led to some understanding of
how humans select sentences, prepare abstracts, and
evaluate the results.*

—H. Borko and C. L. Bernier

Impressionistic Abstracts

The results of "programming the computer to select 'significant representative sentences,'" cited in Borko and Bernier's discussion on computer-based abstracts,[8] not only furnished insights into how humans select sentences from materials to be abstracted, prepare abstracts, and evaluate the results, but also led to some understanding of how well the computer might, in turn, select significant representative sentences and prepare abstracts. Borko and Bernier concluded from their 1975 survey of computer-assisted abstracting systems that the computer may select representative sentences, but it does not yet prepare abstracts—merely extracts.

Evaluation of the content of abstracts in primary scientific and scholarly publications and abstract journals or those on file in data bases would identify a few human-produced extracts that are also mislabeled as abstracts. The relative number of these extracts would serve as one good criterion for estimating the comparative quality of these abstract journals or data bases. At their worst, computer-based and human-prepared extracts that are incorrectly labeled as abstracts are equivalent to a formless, impressionistic printing or typing of sentences on computer printouts or bond paper. At their best, these extracts serve as marginally acceptable substitutes for authentic abstracts.

Shortcomings in computer-based abstracts may be partially traced to the fact that techniques for preparing them have been in the development stage only over the past three decades. Techniques for preparing human abstracts, in contrast, have been developed and refined for at least three centuries. Additionally, unlike the computer, the human has the proved potential to develop the reading, thinking, writing, and editing skills that are prerequisites to the application of these techniques. When applied properly, the advanced techniques available to humans allow them not only to identify representative *sentences* but also to identify representative *information* in whatever form or location it appears in the materials to be abstracted, and to format this information logically, reduce it coherently, and refine it concisely.

Constructing Well-Construed Abstracts

> ... the acts of mind involved in critical reading, in making sense of texts, are the same as those in operation when we compose: how we construe is how we construct.
>
> —ANN E. BERTHOFF[7]

The acts of mind involved in abstracting—in making concise sense of scientific, technical, and scholarly texts—also are based on well-construed elements of composition. The mental acts are performed in four approximate stages: focusing on the basic features of the materials to be abstracted; identifying relevant information; extracting, organizing, and reducing the relevant information into a coherent unit, usually one paragraph long; and refining the completed abstract through editing.

Focusing on basic features.   The first step in the human abstracting process is to determine the general characteristics of the materials to be abstracted—the form, type, size, and structure of the information. The form of the material to be abstracted may be a monograph, article, dissertation, project status report, or letter to the editor, to name a few. Different forms usually require slightly different abstracting procedures.

During the first stage, the materials to be abstracted must be clearly classified by the abstractor. Is the material based on experimental research or testing; epidemiological, etiological, sociological, or psychological surveys; descriptions of methods or equipment; theoretical research or mathematical modeling; or literature reviews, book reviews, or personal views on scientific, technical, or scholarly themes?

How is the text structured? Are primary and secondary headings used, particularly those containing such guide words as "introduction," "methods," "results," "conclusions," and "recommendations," which expedite the locating of representative information for the abstract? Are descriptions of original research readily identifiable, or will there be difficulty in separating them from background information during the succeeding stages of abstracting? For experimental research, are the methods and testing procedures conventional and simple to follow or are they unconventional and complicated? How much generalizing will be necessary to give a balanced, informative treatment in the abstract to the information on purpose, methods, results, conclusions, and recommendations? If there are conclusions, are they presented unambiguously, are they scattered throughout the text, and will they be difficult to separate from the discussion of the work of other investigators?

Before beginning this first stage of abstracting, author abstractors are well aware of these information characteristics. Access abstractors should be able to determine these characteristics in less than two minutes by scanning the materials to be abstracted.

Identifying relevant information.   The second approximate stage in the abstracting process involves a rapid-review reading of the text to identify those portions that contain potentially relevant information for the abstract. (Some abstractors complete this stage simultaneously while focusing on the basic features of the materials during stage 1.)

In a manner similar to the instructions formulated for some test programs that select representative sentences for computer-assisted abstracting, human abstractors seek relevant information through identification of cue words or phrases in sentences in the text ("In this paper we," "Administration of," "Data were analyzed," "Results suggest"). Abstractors also concentrate on the information presented under conventional functional headings such as "Introduction," and "Methods." The location of sentences within paragraphs is also a good indicator of potentially representative information for the abstract. The first or last sentences in a paragraph often are topical or summary ones. Information that is identified through cue or function words and phrases or by locating topical sentences may then be used as a base for identifying additional, less accessible, relevant information that has potential for extraction into the abstract.

Extracting, organizing, and condensing relevant information.   After the most representative information for the abstract has been identified, the abstractor begins the "extracting into abstracting" stage. The extractable information is sorted mentally into a preestablished format. As mentioned, one standard format follows the sequence: purpose, methods, results, conclusions, and recommendations. Other formats generally involve rearrangement of these elements.

Before writing or typing the information for extraction into the abstract in the appropriate sequence, the abstractor reviews it for relevance and validity, and condenses and consolidates it, using cognitive techniques.

Information refinement.   The final stage in human abstracting involves the editing or refining of the raw abstract into a good informative or indicative abstract. The refinement process ranges from minor to major self-editing or revision by author or access abstractors, editors, or reviewers. The following two examples of the editing of lengthy sentences to achieve conciseness were selected from a single abstract that had been reviewed by an editor of access abstracts.

Original version:

There were significant positive associations between the concentrations of the substance administered and mortality in rats and mice of both sexes.

There was no convincing evidence to indicate that endrin ingestion induced any of the different types of tumors which were found in the treated animals.

Edited version:

Mortality in rats and mice of both sexes was dose related.

No treatment-related tumors were found in any of the animals.

Summary of Human Abstracting Process

Figure 4 presents a recapitulation of the approximate stages followed by humans during the abstracting process. Figures 5 and 6 contain two examples of the results of the process.

Stages:	*Techniques:*	*Results:*
1. Focusing on the basic features of the materials to be abstracted	Classifying the form and content of the materials	Determination of the type of abstract to be written, the relative length, and the degree of difficulty
2. Identifying relevant information (sometimes done simultaneously with Stage 1)	(a) Searching for cue or function words and phrases, structural headings and subheadings, and topic sentences; (b) expanding the search based on the results of (a)	Identification of a representative amount of relevant information for extraction
3. Extracting, organizing, and reducing the relevant information	Organizing and writing the extracted relevant information into an abstract, using a standard format	Preparation of a concise, unified, but unedited abstract (see Figure 5)
4. Refining the relevant information	Editing or review of the abstract by the originator or editorial or technical reviewers	Completion of a good informative or indicative abstract (see Figure 6)

FIG. 4. *Approximate stages in the human abstracting process.*

Every cognitive skill draws upon part of the brain's extensive repertoire of representational subsystems, storage mechanisms, and processes. This tutorial article is an introduction to research exploring these basic components of cognitive skill and their organization. Four areas of research are reviewed: the perception of objects and words; the distinction between short- and long-term memory mechanisms; the retrieval of remembered episodes and facts; and attention, performance, and consciousness.

FIG. 5. *Stage 3 abstract.*

Research on the cognitive representational subsystems, storage mechanisms, and processes of the brain is reviewed tutorially. Investigations of the perception of objects and words; short- and long-term memory; the retrieval of remembered episodes and facts; and attention, performance, and consciousness are described.

FIG. 6. *Stage 4 version of the Stage 3 abstract. Adapted from the abstract in Monsell.*[23]

PART II

RETRIEVAL READING
AND RULES

INDICATIVE ABSTRACT:

The importance of analytical reading in the writing of good-quality abstracts is discussed. A three-stage reading method for abstracting is introduced. Stage 1, or retrieval reading, is described, with two sample papers for abstracting. General reading rules for the full abstracting process and specific rules for retrieval reading are presented.

Chapter 5

Analytical Reading and the Three R's of Abstracting

Good, better, best
Never let it rest
Until your good is better
And your better is best.
—ANONYMOUS

Good, Better, and Best Abstracts

What is a good abstract, a better one, or the best one? Many empirical methods and theoretical models have been developed for measuring the quality of abstracts *after* they are written. Most of the results of these measurements are reported in qualified terms because of the many variables in style, content, timeliness, and user requirements that must be considered during the evaluations. Some evaluators claim that the number of variables involved precludes accurate assessments of the quality of abstracts. Although I disagree with this claim, an analysis of its validity is beyond the scope of this book. But to emphasize the primary importance of analytical reading in the abstracting process, I will propose a simple, unqualified "good–better–best" model for predicting the general quality of abstracts *before* they are written.

Good reading skills and habits are commonly accepted as prerequisites for effective writing in any form. Within the simplified good–better–best model for predicting the quality of abstracts, the ability to read analytically is held to be vital throughout the full abstracting process. The analytical reading is preferably done with rules and conventions for abstracting in mind, such as those given in the *American National Standard for Writing Abstracts*, as supplemented by those special instructions on abstracting that have been developed by specific primary publishers or managers of access information systems. Although the most proficient writers of abstracts can perform the reading and writing functions almost simultaneously, I will discuss them separately in this book for clarity of instruction.

The simplified model for predicting the quality of abstracts assumes that only through the development, application, and refinement of good analytical reading skills can good, better, and best abstracts be written, whether by primary authors or professional abstractors. The use of good analytical reading skills combined with average writing and editing skills should result in the preparation of good-quality abstracts; the use of good analytical reading and good writing skills combined with average editing skills should result in the preparation of better-quality abstracts; and the combined use of good analytical reading, writing, and editing skills should result in the preparation of the best-quality abstracts. According to this simple model for predicting the quality of abstracts, failure to develop, apply, and maintain these skills will often result in the preparation of inferior abstracts.

Analytical Reading Skills for Abstracting

Analytical reading for abstracting involves reading actively for information content and passively for understanding during each of three reading stages. (Conversely, reading actively for understanding and passively for information content is more appropriate for research and writing activities that are more complex than abstracting.) In the first or *retrieval reading* stage of abstracting, the abstractor rapidly reads through the full text to locate sections containing relevant information for the abstract on purpose, scope, methods, results, or conclusions and recommendations; in the second or *creative reading* stage, the abstractor rereads the material that was identified during the retrieval stage to select, extract, organize, and write the most relevant information for the abstract. During the final or *critical reading* stage, the abstractor reads the written abstract analytically to edit it for unity and conciseness and to ensure that the pertinent stylistic rules and conventions for abstracting have been complied with fully. (Examples of the application of these analytical reading techniques will be presented in succeeding chapters.)

Very Best Quality Abstracts

As I have stated, the use of good analytical-reading, writing, and editing skills combined with adherence to standard and special rules and conventions for abstracting should result in the preparation of best-quality abstracts. Very best quality abstracts are attainable when the efforts of individual abstractors to *read* analytically and follow *rules* carefully are supported directly or indirectly by cooperative professional *relationships* with other abstractors; with editors, managers, or readers; or with other users of the abstracts. Thus, to paraphrase the more conventional definition of the "three R's," my simple model for predicting the quality of abstracts before they are written is based on the "three R's" of Reading, Rules, and Relationships. Parts II through IV of this book emphasize the importance of "reading" and "rules"; Part V emphasizes the importance of cooperative professional "relationships."

Primary authors of scientific or scholarly materials and candidate or practicing access abstractors who lack confidence in their analytical-reading skills should attempt to obtain formal or informal training in advanced reading techniques. These techniques might include, but should not be limited to, speed reading. For self-instruction in analytical reading, Mortimer Adler's classic guidebook *How to Read a Book*[1] is highly recommended.

The Adler-Van Doren Reading Method

You are told about the various levels of reading and how to achieve them—from elementary reading through systematic skimming and inspectional reading, to speed reading. You learn how to pigeonhole a book, X-ray it, extract the author's message, criticize. You are taught the different reading techniques for reading practical books, imaginative literature, plays, poetry, history, science and mathematics, philosophy and social science.

Mortimer Adler's guidebook on reading was originally published in 1940 and went through many printings before he and Charles Van Doren revised and updated it in 1972.[1] The paragraph that I have inserted above, which was extracted from the text on the back cover of the revised paperback edition, serves well as a short abstract for the book. In my opinion, Chapters 4 through 9 of the book implicitly contain particularly relevant information, advice, and rules on reading in preparation for writing abstracts and on other conventional forms of information analysis, such as indexing, cataloging, and classifying. The later chapters in *How to Read a Book* contain guidance for the reading associated with more complex research assignments such as reviewing, interpreting, and evaluating.

The rules in the early chapters of Adler's book have been used as a guide in compiling the following set of general reading rules for abstractors. Specific rules for retrieval, creative, and critical reading for abstracting will be introduced later.

General Reading Rules for Abstracting

Rule 1.   Read actively to identify information for the abstract and passively for understanding.

Rule 2.   Read with standard rules and conventions and special instructions for writing abstracts in mind.

Rule 3.   Read attentively through the full abstracting process of reading, thinking, writing, and self-editing.

Rule 4.   Read with enthusiasm.

Chapter 6

Retrieval Reading for Sample Abstract A

An abstract should be as informative as is permitted by the type and style of the document; that is, it should present as much as possible of the quantitative or qualitative information contained in the document.
—AMERICAN NATIONAL STANDARD
FOR WRITING ABSTRACTS

In this chapter and the following one, I apply the rules for retrieval reading to two sample papers for abstracting. These papers then are used to illustrate the creative-reading stage for the writing of abstracts (Part III) and the critical-reading stage for the self-editing of abstracts (Part IV).

The first sample article is a paper on experimental research that appeared in the *Journal of Physical Chemistry*.[17] The discussion of the abstracting process for this article is directed primarily toward authors of papers and monographs who must prepare their own abstracts and secondarily to access abstractors, particularly those who are in training to become abstractors. The second sample, which is a review of a book on the modeling of urban systems, is discussed in Chapter 7.

The sample articles were selected chiefly for their diversity of information content, short to moderate length, and potential for demonstrating different forms of abstracts, since they had been previously abstracted both by humans and by a computer-assisted abstracting system. These forms will be shown in Part IV within the discussion of the critical-reading stage for the self-editing of abstracts.

Before beginning the discussion of sample abstract A, I will draw an analogy to the sport of golf to illustrate the diversity in form and the complexity in content of the materials that are abstracted. The type and total number of abstracts written by a prolific researcher over the course of a productive career or by a professional abstractor in a highly productive day's work might figuratively parallel the experience of a low-

25

handicap golfer playing a round of golf on an 18-hole golf course. As with some of the golf holes, some of the 18 items to be abstracted will be lengthy and complex with a high potential for stymieing the abstractor. These will require the use of the highest skills, concentration, and energy to achieve good (par), better (birdie), or best (eagle) abstracting (playing) results. Others of the items to be abstracted will be short and simple, permitting the author or access abstractor to go straight to the point quickly and smoothly in a minimum number of strokes of the typewriter or the pen.

Retrieval-Reading Rules

There are two rules for retrieval reading. They should be observed in conjunction with the general reading rules given in Chapter 5. Retrieval reading is ideally done once, non-stop, with a minimum of regressions and fixations. In practice, it may be necessary to repeat portions of this reading process.

Rule 1.   Read quickly but attentively through the text of the material to be abstracted to identify passages containing information with potential for inclusion in the abstract.

Rule 2.   While reading, mentally or in the margin of the copy note which parts of the material contain information on purpose, methods, findings, or conclusions and recommendations. (If you mark in the margins on manuscripts or published copies of materials being abstracted, write lightly in pencil so that the markings may be erased without damaging the copy.)

Retrieval Reading for Sample Abstract A

The results of applying retrieval-reading rules 1 and 2 to the text of the first sample article follow. The vertical symbols in the left-hand margins denote paragraphs or tables containing background (●), purpose, scope, and methods (▶), results (□), and conclusions and recommendations (▷). The actual writing of the abstract for this article is discussed in Chapter 9.

Sample Article A*

Introduction

Reactions below about 150°K in the oxygen atom–olefin system occur without the formation of fragmentation products. A very decided advantage to studies in this temperature region is that the distinction between concurrent reaction paths characterized by small energy differences is emphasized. An example is provided in the comparison of the reactions of *cis*- and *trans*-2-butenes with O(^{3}P) at 90°K. *cis*-2-Butene gives approximately equal quantities of *cis*- and *trans*-2,3-epoxybutane. Of the epoxybutanes produced from *trans*-2-butene, 90% are *trans*.[1,2] It is well established that oxygen atom addition to olefins gives carbonyls as well as epoxides.[1,3] Carbonyl compounds can arise only by rearrangements in which either a hydrogen atom or an alkyl group is shifted from its original position on one of the olefinic carbon atoms. Both rearrangement processes, namely, the change of configuration in the epoxides from that of the parent olefin and the migration of a hydrogen atom or an alkyl group, are amenable to observation by previously developed, low-temperature methods. Several olefins were selected for study of the O atom addition to illuminate the nature of these rearrangements.

Straight-Chain, Internal Olefins

The addition of O(^{3}P) to straight-chain, internal olefins is interesting because of *cis–trans* isomerism in the olefin and in the resulting epoxide compounds. A consideration of the O atom addition to *cis*- and *trans*-2-butene in the temperature region 77 to 113°K led to the formulation of a new transition intermediate.[2] In this intermediate, the oxygen atom is represented as bound in a loose, three-membered ring with, and in the plane of, the olefinic structure of the reactant. An interaction between the oxygen atom and the adjacent hydrogen atoms bonded to the olefinic carbon atoms is also postulated. The necessity for the as-

* Reprinted from R. Klein and M. D. Scheer, *Journal of Physical Chemistry* 74(3):613–616, 1970. Published by the American Chemical Society.

sumption of this interaction arises from the observation that, for both *cis-* and *trans-*2-butene, the ratio of *cis-*2,3-epoxybutane to isobutyraldehyde, as well as that of *trans-*2,3-epoxybutane to 2-butanone, remains constant. The relationship holds over a wide temperature range (77–300°K), despite large differences in the ratios of *trans-* to *cis-*2,3-epoxybutane produced from *cis-* compared to *trans-*2-butene (1.25–8.3). Observations on 2-butenes have been extended to several more straight-chain, internal olefins in the low-temperature region. The results are given in Table I. Comparison of the *trans-*epoxide to ketone ratios from the *cis-* *vs.* the *trans-*olefin with increasing size of the olefin indicates that these ratios diverge. However, the larger olefins show greater stereospecificity in their reactions. Thus, *cis-*3-hexene gives about 2.5 times as much *cis-*3,4-epoxyhexane as the *trans-*epoxide. Even a relatively small quantity of 3-hexanone from the *cis* intermediate could easily account for the difference in the *trans-*epoxide/ketone ratio between the reactions of *cis-* and *trans-*3-hexene. It is noted that the recently proposed "epoxide-like" transition complex implies that, although only one form of the complex is possible from the *trans-*, two forms are possible from the *cis-*olefin

Of these, form b could readily lead to the ketone, because of easy migration of H, but form a would be expected to preponderate from the energetic viewpoint.

An indication of the importance of these forms, within the framework of the transition states specified and the assumption that form a gives only the aldehyde in its rearrangement to the carbonyl end product, whereas form b gives mostly ketones, is obtained from the data of Table I. The *trans-*olefin compounds, as may be noted, produce epoxides that contain 90–97% of the *trans* form. If the same ratio of *cis-*epoxide to aldehyde obtained from the *cis-*3-hexene is maintained in the *trans-*3-hexene products, the residual aldehyde presumed to arise from the *trans* intermediate may be calculated. Accordingly a ratio of 50:1 for the *trans-*epoxide/aldehyde compounds derived

● Background information
▶ Purpose, scope, and methods

Table I: Fractional Product Yields for the O(^{3}P) Addition to Internal, Straight-Chain Olefins at 90°K[a]

Products	2-Butene		2-Pentene		3-Hexene		4-Octene	
	cis	*trans*	*cis*	*trans*	*cis*	*trans*	*cis*	*trans*
trans-Epoxide	0.30	0.50	0.26	0.59	0.17	0.65	0.09	0.68
cis-Epoxide	0.24	0.06	0.34	0.04	0.42	0.02	0.82[c]	0.03[c]
Aldehyde	0.21	0.06	0.20[b]	0.04	0.28	0.03		
Ketone	0.25	0.38	0.20[b]	0.33[b]	0.13	0.30	0.09	0.29
trans-Epoxide/ketone	1.2	1.3	1.3	1.8	1.3	2.2	1.0	2.3
cis-Epoxide/aldehyde	1.1	1.0	1.7	1.0	1.5	0.7		
cis-Epoxide/*trans*-epoxide	0.8	0.12	1.3	0.07	2.5	0.03		
Total epoxide/total carbonyl	1.2	1.3	1.5	1.7	1.4	2.0		

[a] The olefins were diluted 10:1 in propane prior to condensation on a 100-cm² Pyrex surface. [b] Sum of 2-pentanone and 3-pentanone, not separated on the glpc. [c] Sum of 2-propylpentanal and *cis*-4,5-epoxyoctane, not separated on the glpc.

□ □ □ □ □ □ ▲ ▲

□ Results
▷ Conclusions and recommendations

☐ from the *trans* complex is obtained. Clearly, aldehyde
▷ formation from the *trans* intermediate is negligible. All
▷ of the straight-chain olefins of Table I conform to
▷ this generalization. The *trans*-epoxide/ketone ratio
☐ obtained from the *cis*- as compared to the *trans*-olefin
☐ shows the largest difference with 4-octene. The cor-
▷ rect value, 2.3, is obtained from *trans*-4-octene, because
▷ a contribution from the *cis* complex possible is virtually
◀ absent. This factor was used to calculate the ketone
◀ residual from the *cis* complex, starting with the *cis*-
▷ 4-octene. Although the *cis*-epoxide and aldehyde were
▷ not separated, the ratio of the two may be assumed
▷ to be the same as the corresponding one from *cis*-3-
☐ hexene. The aldehyde/ketone ratio resulting from
☐ the *cis*-4-octene–oxygen complex is calculated to be
▷ about 7. It may be concluded that of the two forms
▷ of the transition complex derived from the *cis*-olefin,
▷ form a is the principal one and b is unimportant.

④ ▷   Two generalizations are apparent from Table I.
▷ The first is that retention of configuration of products
▷ becomes more pronounced with increasing chain length
▷ of the olefin. The second is that reaction of oxygen
▷ atoms in the low-temperature region tends to be more
▷ stereospecific with *trans*- than with *cis*-olefins. A
▷ stereotransformation of the transition intermediate re-
▷ quires a rotation of 180°, about the modified olefinic
▷ bond, of one of the carbon atoms of the double bond
▷ with its attached groups. Obviously, this process
▷ occurs with the *cis*-olefins. The extent to which
▷ stereotransformation will occur depends on the rates
▷ of ring closure and the rates of rearrangements leading
▷ to final products, compared to the rate of the *cis–*
▷ *trans* interchange in the complex. It seems reasonable
▷ to postulate that the rate of ring closure is independent
▷ of the size of the olefin. The ratio of total epoxide
▷ to total carbonyl products shows little change with
▷ size, and, hence, the rate of rearrangement to carbonyls
▷ is also size independent. The frequency of rotation
▷ of the portion of the complex

▷ is then directly proportional to the extent of stereotrans-
▷ formation observed in the products. A measure of
▷ these transformations is the ratio of *cis*- to *trans*-
● epoxide, tabulated in Table I. In a rotationally un-
● hindered system, the frequency is inversely related

● Background information
▶ Purpose, scope, and methods

to the moment of inertia of the rotating group. Qualitatively, it would be expected that because of the higher moment of inertia associated with the larger olefin, the stereospecificity should increase with size; this is indeed the case. It is interesting that *cis*-2-pentene shows more stereospecificity than *cis*-2-butene. Despite the fact that both compounds have a methyl group adjacent to the olefinic site, a larger rotational barrier is inferred to be associated with the 2-pentene. A quantitative consideration of the relationship of size and stereo effects would require that potential barriers for rotation be taken into account also, but the qualitative conclusions remain unaffected.

Group Migrations

Carbonyl compounds constitute a sizable fraction of the products of the oxygen atom addition to olefins in the low-temperature region and, as has been noted, an intramolecular group migration is required for carbonyl formation. The principal carbonyl product in the *trans*-2-butene reaction at 90°K is 2-butanone. The formation of this ketone requires the migration of H. Compared to migration .. the methyl group, that of H is highly favored. *cis*-2-Butene is not useful for the comparison, as both of the hydrogen atoms attached to the olefinic carbon pair are suppressed through interaction with oxygen in the complex. The relative quantities of 2-butanone to isobutyraldehyde, after correction of the latter for the contribution from the *cis* complex, is taken as a measure of the ratio of migration of the hydrogen atom to migration of the methyl group. At 90°K, it is about 30. Similar considerations for *trans*-3-hexene lead to a value of about 20 for the ratio of migration of hydrogen with respect to the ethyl group. If rates of migration are independent quantities, to be associated with the specific groups, the rate of migration of ethyl should be the same as, or slightly higher than, that of the methyl group. These ratios are imprecise, because of the small quantities of the aldehyde produced in each case. A direct comparison between methyl and ethyl migrations is desirable if their relative rates are to be established; this can be done through the use of 3,4-dimethyl-3-hexene (DMH). The O(^{3}P) reaction gives, in addition to 3,4-epoxy-3,4-dimethylhexane, two ketones, namely, 4,4-dimethyl-3-hexanone and 3-ethyl-3-methyl-2-pentanone, depending on whether the methyl or ethyl group migrates. The reaction gives no other products.

▶ Both *cis*- and *trans*-3,4-dimethyl-3-hexene were used.
The two ketone products, 4,4-dimethyl-3-hexanone
and 3-ethyl-3-methyl-2-pentanone, will be referred to
as I and II. The use of 3-ethyl-2-methyl-2-pentene
(MEP) furnishes further data for assessing the validity
of the concept of relative rates of migration of groups
in establishing the product ratios.

☐ The same two ketones are produced from MEP as
☐ from *cis*- and *trans*-DMH. The important difference

● Background information
▶ Purpose, scope, and methods

is that, whereas I results from the reactions of DMH with a rearrangement wherein a methyl group migrates, it is the migration of the ethyl group that gives I from MEP. Ketone II results from ethyl migration starting withD MH, or methyl migration starting with MEP. Therefore, if independent rates of migration are to be associated with these alkyl groups, the ketone ratio (I/II) produced from *cis-* or *trans-* DMH should be equal to (II/I) formed from MEP. It is emphasized that this follows if the presumed migration rates determine the position at which the O, becomes localized. On the other hand, strong forces favoring addition to one of the olefinic carbons could control the alkyl group migrations.

Reactions were effected at 90°K in the apparatus routinely used for this purpose.[1] The olefins were diluted 10 to 1 with propane. The exposure time to oxygen atoms was 5 min, and about 1% of the olefin was reacted. The products were determined, after warmup, on a column (0.25 in. × 12 ft glpc) of Carbowax-6000, at 135° and a helium flow of 100 cc/min. The *cis* and *trans* isomers of 3,4-epoxy-3,4-dimethyl-hexane were not separable. Ketones I and II were easily separable. Retention times were determined with authentic samples of the two ketones. For all three olefins, only three glpc peaks were obtained for the products. These corresponded to the epoxides and the ketones I and II. Ratios of yield of product from oxygen atom addition are given in Table II.

The notable feature of these results is that, of the two ketones, I and II, I is the major product; (I/II) = 2.5:1. Furthermore, this ratio is virtually independent of the starting olefin. Thus, the concept of independent rates of migration of groups in the rearrangement occurring in the O atom addition to olefins *must be abandoned.* The other alternative would require that the directive effect of the alkyl groups in MEP is such that the O adds to the carbon with the two ethyl groups 2.5 times more rapidly than to the carbon with the two methyl groups. It would appear that, insofar as the ratio of ketones is concerned, it is their relative stabilities that control the rearrangement processes. Transformation to final products is a migration of an alkyl group concerted with the localization of the oxygen atom on one of the carbon atoms. Localization of the oxygen atom in the transition complex *preceding* alkyl group rearrangement is not in accord with the experimental results. If, in fact, localization did occur,

☐ Results
▷ Conclusions and recommendations

the migration would be determined, in part (completely,

Table II: Product Yield Ratios for the O(^{3}P) Addition to Some Isomeric Octenes at 90°K

	Product ratios	
Reactant	Ketone ratio (I/II)	Epoxides/ ketones
cis-DMH	2.5	1.9
trans-DMH	2.7	1.1
MEP	2.6	2.4

if, as in MEP, the groups bonded to each of the olefinic carbon atoms occurred in pairs), by the directive factors, such as electron densities that are postulated as controlling the site of addition.   It has been previously stated that oxygen atoms add mainly to the less-substituted carbon atom and that a methyl group confers "less substitution" than an ethyl group.[4]   The directive influence of ethyl vs. methyl has been noted[5] for hydrogen atom addition to 2-pentene.   At 90°K, the ratio of addition to C-2 is 1.6 times that to C-3. For MEP, addition of the O atom to that carbon atom of the double bond to which the two methyl groups are would, perforce, be formed in greater amounts than I; the data show unequivocally that this is incorrect.

The concerted rearrangement, in which oxygen localization and group migration occur, requires both electronic and spatial reorganization.   The addition of ground-state, triplet oxygen to singlet-state olefin to give singlet-state products requires a relaxation process, as represented by a crossing of states on a potential surface.   The recently introduced representation of the initial transition intermediate as a loose epoxide structure seems especially appropriate.   Migration of groups probably involves a transient bridging of the double bond carbon pair.   The path by which the intermediate relaxes to final products could even involve steric effects.   The formation of the grouping

$$-C\!\!\begin{array}{c} C_2H_5 \\ -C_2H_5 \\ CH_3 \end{array}$$

in II is sterically less favorable than

$$-C\!\!\begin{array}{c} CH_3 \\ -CH_3 \\ C_2H_5 \end{array}$$

● Background information
▶ Purpose, scope, and methods

▷ in I, and it may be speculated that the preponderance of
▷ I over II in the reactions of the *cis*- and *trans*-DMH and
▷ MEP can be ascribed to such steric effects.

⑨ ▷   Table II shows an interesting variation among the
▷ three olefins as regards the epoxide/ketone ratio.   The
▷ interpretation of these results, and, particularly, why
▷ MEP exhibits such a high epoxide/ketone ratio, is not
▷ yet at hand.

☐ **Results**
▷ **Conclusions and recommendations**

Chapter 7

Retrieval Reading for Sample
Abstract B

*Readers for whom the document is of fringe interest often
obtain enough information from the abstract to make
their reading of the whole document unnecessary.
Therefore, every primary document should include a good
abstract.*

—AMERICAN NATIONAL STANDARD
FOR WRITING ABSTRACTS

Differences in Reading Done
by Author and Access Abstractors

The discussion of retrieval reading for sample abstract B is directed primarily to access abstractors and secondarily to authors who furnish abstracts with some of their scientific, technical, or scholarly writing. Access abstractors differ from primary authors who write their own abstracts in the speed with which they abstract, their relative objectivity, and the diversity of the materials that they abstract.

The access abstractor normally writes abstracts to meet more stringent deadlines than those of author abstractors and, therefore, must read at a faster rate. The access abstractor reads the material that he is abstracting from "the outside in," since he comes to it completely unaware of its contents. Reading from "the inside out," the author is thoroughly familiar with the contents and may even subjectively apply the results of his reading for abstracting to further modify the materials in his text. The access abstractor must remain completely objective throughout the abstracting process (unless he or she is preparing a critical abstract—a type of abstract seldom published in recent years). The access abstractor also routinely abstracts a diverse selection of materials, many of which are normally only abstracted for secondary publications and information-retrieval systems. The article selected for the writing of sample abstract B is one such paper.

Retrieval Reading for Sample Abstract B

The two retrieval-reading rules given in Chapter 6, along with the general reading rules given in Chapter 5, have been applied to an article that was initially published in *Fortune*[16] without an abstract. The article is a critical review of a monograph on models for urban planning. Again, symbols have been inserted in the margin to designate passages in the review article containing information of potential relevance to the abstract. These are ● (background information), ▶ (purpose and scope or depth of coverage), and □ (conclusions and recommendations). The actual writing of the abstract for this article is discussed in Chapter 10.

Sample Article B*

The intense interest in the problems of the cities in recent years has produced a great outpouring of books diagnosing and proposing remedies for the "urban crisis." The majority of these works are hardly noticed, being undistinguished and rather pallid imitations of one another. Jay W. Forrester's *Urban Dynamics* (M.I.T. Press) stands out in all this verbiage. The book has attracted attention because of the unorthodoxy of Forrester's recommendations, the self-assured manner in which he presents them, and his prominent use of the prestigious tools of systems analysis. With so many insistent voices saying that cities need more financial help from state and federal government, readers are likely to be impressed with Forrester's conclusion that help from the outside may "worsen conditions" in cities. Forrester, moreover, makes it difficult for readers to argue with him. With its appearance of rigor and scientism, its charts and diagrams, its arrays of numbers printed out by a computer, *Urban Dynamics* is rather intimidating.

Forrester, a professor at M.I.T.'s Sloan School of Management, relies on a computer model he developed to simulate the growth, decline, and stagnation of a hypothetical city (or "urban area") from birth to old age (250 years). Such methods have a great deal of potential for the analysis of urban problems and have already demonstrated their value in a number of specific, though limited applications. However, the development of truly useful and trustwor-

* Reprinted by permission from "A Computer Version of How a City Works" by John F. Kain. Published by *Fortune*. Copyright 1969 by *Fortune*,

thy urban simulation models remains a distant objective and will require much greater resources than have yet been devoted to the task. Before adequate models become available, many inadequate ones will be put forward. Forrester's model is a conspicuous example. In his first chapter Forrester warns the reader that caution should be exercised in applying the model to actual situations. Subsequently, however, he expresses few reservations about the model's validity and freely uses it as a basis for prescribing public policy.

A goal of minimum taxes

The hypothetical city in *Urban Dynamics* is, in Forrester's words, "a system of interacting industries, housing, and people." At the start of the simulations there is only new industry in the city, but as time passes enterprises mature and then decline. The speed of this aging process depends on conditions in the city. As businesses pass through these successive stages, they employ fewer workers and a smaller proportion of skilled workers.

There are similarly three kinds of people in the city: "managerial-professional," "labor" (skilled or high-income workers), and "underemployed" (including unemployed and unskilled workers). And there are three kinds of housing, corresponding to the three kinds of people: premium housing, worker housing, and underemployed housing.

The criteria used in evaluating the performance of the hypothetical city and the efficacy of alternative public policies are never explicitly set forth. However, minimization of taxes per capita would be a fair rendering of the underlying criteria. Forrester seems to think that the objective of the city is to produce the lowest possible tax rate.

The fiscal relationships in Forrester's urban system are intricate, but can be reduced to three fairly simple propositions: (1) Low-

● Background information

▶ Purpose and scope or depth of coverage

☐ Conclusions and recommendations

income households cost the city more in taxes than they pay, whereas the city makes a profit on high-income households. (2) Growing business enterprises are an unqualified good because they pay taxes and, by assumption, cost the city nothing in services. (3) Increases in local taxes and increases in local government expenditures produce "adverse" changes in the city's population and employment structure. It follows from these propositions that "urban-management policies" should be designed to encourage new enterprises and managerial-professional people to locate in the city and discourage low-skilled people from living there.

(7) The influence of tax rates on employment and population structure in Forrester's city is powerful and pervasive. "Managerial-professional" and "labor" families are assumed to be repelled by high tax rates, whereas the "underemployed" are indifferent to them. High tax rates, moreover, discourage the formation of new enterprises and accelerate the aging of existing ones. There are still other adverse effects: high taxes retard construction of both premium and worker housing, which in turn discourages the kinds of people who live in these kinds of housing from moving to the city or remaining there.

(8) Increases in public expenditures, the other half of the local fiscal equation, also have disastrous effects on the system. It is assumed that increases in expenditures per capita make the city no more attractive to high-income people and new enterprises, but make it substantially more attractive to low-income people. There are some small offsets in the positive effects of higher expenditures per capita on upward mobility from the underemployed class into the labor class; but these are overwhelmed by the direct and indirect effects on the size of the underemployed population.

(9) These examples are only a few of the "ad-

verse" consequences of higher taxes and increased public expenditures in Forrester's model. Since the model is so constructed that a development in one sector affects other sectors, these adverse effects cumulate throughout the system.

Help from an induced shortage

(10) Forrester uses his simulation model to evaluate several "urban-management programs" that have been tried or proposed, and he concludes that they "may actually worsen the conditions they are intended to improve." For example, he finds that "financial support from the outside"—presumably including revenue sharing by the federal government—"may do nothing to improve fundamental conditions within the city and may even worsen conditions in the long run." But this conclusion is not at all surprising in view of what he does with the outside funds. Rather than using them to reduce or hold down city taxes, as proponents of such intergovernment transfers envision, Forrester uses them to increase city expenditures. Given the framework of his model, the net effects are inevitably adverse. If instead Forrester had used the outside support to reduce city taxes, the net effects would have been favorable to the hypothetical city. Virtually all of Forrester's evaluations of "conventional" policies are similarly flawed; none is a faithful rendering of policies it supposedly represents.

(11) Considering the heavy emphasis Forrester puts on tax rates, it is striking that he fails to consider the costs of his principal recommendation: each year demolish 5 percent of the low-income housing. The costs of acquiring and demolishing the properties would increase city taxes, and, within the framework of the model, any increase in city taxes has adverse effects. But Forrester considers only the favorable effects of the demolition program. Given his model, these are considerable. The induced short-

● Background
information

▶ Purpose and
scope or
depth of coverage

☐ Conclusions and
recommendations

age of low-income housing makes the city less attractive to low-income people; fewer come and more leave. (Where they go is a question the model is not designed to consider.) As before, a decline in the ratio of "underemployed" to total population makes the city more attractive to high-income people, encourages formation of new enterprises and construction of premium and worker housing, and impedes deterioration of dwelling units and businesses. In addition, the land cleared by increased demolition of low-income housing provides space for new enterprises and for premium and worker housing.

(12) The supply of vacant land is a critical variable in Forrester's urban model. When more than half the land is still vacant, using additional land produces increasingly favorable effects. But once half the land in the city has been put to use—which in the simulations occurs at about 100 years—further depletions produce increasingly adverse effects. The city's growth is retarded, and stagnation and decline begin. As more land is used up, the scarcity of vacant land slows formation of new enterprises and construction of premium and worker housing, and speeds obsolescence of both enterprises and housing. Given the critical role of land availability in the model, it would appear that these adverse effects could be staved off if the city could simply extend its boundaries so as to absorb additional vacant land; but Forrester does not deal with this possibility.

Where the solution lies

(13) Simplification is essential in computer simulation models, and neither Forrester's nor any other model can be criticized merely because it omits detail. But Forrester omits some basic behavioral relationships. The model's most serious weakness is that the suburbs never explicitly appear in it. For some simulation purposes, it might be

permissible to disregard temporarily the interrelations between, say, the city and the rest of the nation beyond the metropolitan area. But what happens in a city strongly influences its suburbs, and vice versa. If the central city reduced its low-income population by 100,000, the low-income population of the suburbs would have to increase by roughly the same amount. Although Forrester's model reflects no awareness of this aspect of metropolitan interdependence, suburban governments are all too aware of it. Indeed, much of the urban problem today is a result of suburban governments' successfully pursuing precisely the kind of beggar-thy-neighbor policies Forrester advocates for the central city.

(14) Upon scrutiny, *Urban Dynamics* amounts to an intricate attempt to justify the responses of big-city mayors to a harsh fiscal environment. Existing intergovernmental arrangements saddled them with awesome responsibilities for the nation's social problems, but failed to provide them with commensurate financial resources. Much of the mayors' enthusiasm for now much-criticized urban-renewal programs is traceable to their desperate need for cash. In *Urban Dynamics*, pragmatic responses to an unbalanced allocation of responsibilities and tax resources are elevated to the status of rational and efficient policies for dealing with the complex web of problems popularly referred to as the "urban crisis."

(15) The solution is not, as Forrester indicates, the pursuance of narrow self-interest by each local government. Instead we need to develop a more appropriate division of responsibilities and functions among governments, and thereby remove the fiscal incentives for local governments to follow policies that, while perhaps efficient from the viewpoint of narrow self-interest, are inefficient from the viewpoint of society as a whole.   END

● Background information

▶ Purpose and scope or depth of coverage

☐ Conclusions and recommendations

PART III

CREATIVE READING AND RULES

INDICATIVE ABSTRACT:

Creative reading, the second of the three stages of analytical reading for abstracting, is described. Rules for creative reading are applied to the writing of two sample abstracts. The length and style of abstracts are discussed, as well as the time required to write them.

Chapter 8

Creative Reading for Abstracting

But the main errors in his writing
Are those common in his reading.
—H. J. Tɪᴄʜʏ

Writing Skills for Abstracting

Henrietta Tichy, in her guidebook *Effective Writing: For Engineers, Managers, and Scientists,*[30] instructs "the professional man who is eager to write better" primarily in the fundamentals of writing and secondarily in those of reading so that he can "grasp the philosophy of style and apply the techniques with imagination and originality." The instructions in this part of this book are concerned with grasping and applying the principles of creative reading with imagination and originality to become a good writer of abstracts.

I assume that most readers of this book either already have a sound grasp of the fundamentals of scientific, technical, and scholarly writing or, if not, that they are willing to supplement the knowledge on the broader principles of such writing that they may gain from reading this text with more specialized training in writing skills through either formal or self-instruction courses.

For those with proved writing skills, the transition to writing abstracts should be a smooth, but not necessarily an effortless, one. Just as the athlete who is proficient in using the eye and hand skills necessary for playing competitive tennis has a head start if he decides to take up other racket sports, such as table tennis, squash, or racketball, so also does the individual with proved reading and writing skills in other writing forms have a head start in writing abstracts. His abstracts are not likely to be winning ones, however, until he learns and applies the methods and rules for writing them. For those whose writing skills in scientific and scholarly literature are still in the early stages of development, the materials in this part of the book will be broadly beneficial. By themselves, however, they are not guaranteed miraculously to transform many, if any, novices into

47

polished writers. For this to happen, more comprehensive formal courses or self-instruction in writing techniques is advisable, combined with practical experience and the advice of proficient writers and good editors.

Creative Reading—So What's That?

Creative reading, the second stage of analytical reading for abstracting, is a method of compressing the "what's what" purpose, findings, conclusions, and recommendations information that was discovered during the retrieval reading stage into the most essential, or "so what is *most* important?" information. This information is then creatively extracted and written into a concise unified abstract.

During the final or critical reading stage to be discussed in Part IV, the abstractor carefully reads the completed abstract to refine further its content and style. The resulting abstract should satisfy the "this is what" requirement of a good informative abstract. Now the abstractor may confidently state: *"This is what* I think is the most informative and most terse abstract possible for this document, considering the constraints of time, length, rules, conventions, and special instructions on style and content under which it was written."

Creative-Reading Rules

There are four rules for creative reading for writing abstracts. They are given below. In the next two chapters, they are used to write illustrative abstracts for the two sample papers that were introduced in Part II.

Rule 1. (*Step A*) Reread all of the information on purpose, scope, and methods that you identified during the retrieval-reading process. While reading, mentally index the primary and secondary themes described in this material, using your own choice of arbitrary terms or phrases. (Beginning abstractors or those writing an abstract for a complex document might find it helpful to jot down their arbitrary index terms or phrases on note paper.) (*Step B*) Write the primary annotative part of the abstract (the first sentence).

Rule 2. From the remaining information on purpose, scope, and methods, extract appropriate materials and write the secondary annotative sentence or sentences.

If your instructions are to write an indicative abstract, you have now completed the creative-reading stage and are ready to begin the critical-reading stage for self-editing of the completed abstract. If you are writing an informative abstract, continue on to Rules 3 and 4.

Rule 3.   (*Step A*) If you are writing an abstract of a document reporting on experimental research, tests, surveys, or case reports, reread the textual materials on the results or findings. While reading, condense this information mentally or write it on note paper, to aid your judgment of its relevance and significance. (*Step B*) Extract the most relevant results and write them in sentence form, concisely, in descending order of significance.

Rule 4.   (*Step A*) Reread the conclusions and recommendations that were identified during the retrieval-reading process in a manner similar to that described in Rule 3. (*Step B*) Extract the most relevant conclusions and recommendations and write them in sentence form, tersely, in descending order of significance. (Application of this rule depends on whether it is required by publishers or managers of access-information systems.)

Chapter 9

Creative Reading for Sample Abstract A

*I always have two things in my head—I always have a
theme and the form. The form looks for the theme, the
theme looks for the form, and when they come together
you're able to write.*

—W. H. AUDEN

During the retrieval-reading process discussed in Chapter 6, the purpose, scope, methods, results, and conclusions "themes" for the writing of the abstract for sample paper A were identified. Applying the rules of creative reading, I will now write an informative abstract for this paper. But first, I will briefly discuss some matters relating to the "themes and forms" of abstracts.

Length of Abstracts

Although some primary publishers or contractors for access information services specify the exact length that abstracts should take ("150 words," "200 words," etc.), most specifications for the length of abstracts are properly less specific ("approximately 150 words," "in 200 words or less"). The more general instructions are more appropriate because the length is mainly a function of the type and content of the information contained in the material being abstracted. The *American National Standard for Writing Abstracts* uses the qualifier "fewer" when recommending the number of words to be used:

> For most papers and portions of monographs, an abstract of fewer
> than 250 words will be adequate. For notes and short communica-
> tions, fewer than 100 words should suffice.

Mary-Claire van Leunen in *A Handbook for Scholars*[31] measures the length of abstracts in minutes of reading time: "In fact, a good device for writing abstracts is to pretend that you're in a phone booth, making a long-distance call to a colleague. You want to give him the gist of your latest paper, and you have change for only three minutes." The three minutes of time should be more than adequate for reading the content of most abstracts. For many abstracts, the author should even have enough time left over in the phone call after reading the abstract to mention the status of his current research and future plans.

Style of Abstracts

> That style is best in an abstract which more *quickly* conveys the necessary information. Clarity is essential; vividness is not.... Brevity is important but is to be measured by the amount of information conveyed in a given space, not by the number of lines.

Borko and Chatman[9] quoted the above instructions on style from the policies and procedures for *Psychological Abstracts* in their 1963 survey of abstractors' instructions, which was done to develop a set of criteria for judging the adequacy of an abstract.

Concern for the structure, style, and content of abstracts is important during both the writing and self-editing phases of abstracting. But further discussion on these matters will be deferred (see Chapter 11) until provisional versions of the two sample abstracts have been written and discussed in this and the next chapter.

Creative Reading of Sample Paper A, Rule 1

With the general rules and conventions for writing an informative abstract in mind, I will now begin to write the abstract for sample paper A. Step A of Rule 1 for creative reading states: *Reread all of the information on purpose, scope, and methods that you identified during the retrieval-reading process. While reading, mentally index the primary and secondary themes described in this material, using your own choice of arbitrary terms. (Beginning abstractors or those writing an abstract for a complex document might find it helpful to jot down their arbitrary index terms on note paper.)*

During the retrieval reading of sample paper A, information on purpose, scope, and methods was located, either explicitly or implicitly, in five of the nine paragraphs (1–3, 5, and 6) and one of the two tables (Table I) in the paper. In the extracts of two of these paragraphs below, I have inserted arbitrary index terms in brackets at the end of each paragraph. This is a convenient way to illustrate this procedure, but it is too formalized and time-consuming to be recommended for general practice. Mental indexing or the jotting down of the arbitrary terms or phrases informally on note paper is preferable.

[Paragraph 1] Both rearrangement processes, namely, the change of configuration in the epoxides from that of the parent olefin and the migration of a hydrogen atom or an alkyl group, are amenable to observation by previously developed, low-temperature methods. Several olefins were selected for study of the O atom addition to illuminate the nature of these rearrangements. [INDEX TERMS: rearrangements, epoxide configuration, hydrogen atom or alkyl group migration, low temperature]

[Paragraph 2] The addition of $O(^3P)$ to straight-chain, internal olefins is interesting because of *cis–trans* isomerism in the olefin and in the resulting epoxide compounds. A consideration of the O atom addition to *cis*- and *trans*-2-butene in the temperature region 77 to 113°K led to formulation of a new transition intermediate. In this intermediate, the oxygen atom is represented as bound in a loose, three-membered ring with, and in the plane of, the olefinic structure of the reactant. An interaction between the oxygen atom and the adjacent hydrogen atoms bonded to the olefinic carbon atoms is also postulated. . . . Observations on 2-butenes have been extended to several more straight-chain, internal olefins in the low-temperature region. [INDEX TERMS: *cis-trans* isomerism, epoxides, 2-butene, straight-chain, internal olefins, low temperature, transition intermediate]

The extracts of these two paragraphs on the information on purpose, scope, and methods in sample paper A should adequately demonstrate the first step in Rule 1 of the creative-reading process. This closer analysis through creative reading permits access abstractors to grasp the information content of the paragraphs more thoroughly and aids author abstractors in identifying clearly those details in their work that are relevant for consideration during the writing of the first sentence of the abstract (Rule 1, Step B). No further extracts from the paper for this part of the abstract will be given here. A more complete version of the results of the critical-reading and arbitrary-indexing process for abstract A is provided in Appendix 5.

Creative-Reading Rule 1, Step B

The second step in Rule 1 for creative reading covers the writing of the first or primary annotative sentence of the abstract based on the results of rereading and weighing the relative significance of the information on purpose, scope, and methods in the sample paper. The writing process involves conventional logical and grammatical techniques. The mechanics of these techniques are discussed broadly in other places in this text or are inferred in the makeup of the sentences prepared for sample abstracts

A and B in this and the following chapter and in the other examples of abstracts included in the text, particularly those in Chapter 15.

As often happens, the introductory material in paragraph 1 of the paper contains the most significant leads for completion of this step. This material, supplemented by other information on purpose, scope, and methods in the other four paragraphs and in Table I, was used to write the following primary annotative sentence.

> The effects of oxygen atom addition to olefins on epoxide configuration rearrangements and migration of hydrogen and methyl and ethyl groups were studied at 90°K by using gas-liquid paper chromatography.

Secondary Annotation—Rule 2

From the remaining information on purpose, scope, and methods, extract appropriate materials and write the secondary annotative sentence or sentences.

For many short abstracts, or for longer ones in which the information on purpose, scope, and methods is covered adequately in the first sentence, this rule is inapplicable. Two secondary annotative sentences are, however, proposed for sample abstract A:

> *Cis–trans* isomerism in straight-chain, internal olefins and resulting epoxide compounds was determined. *Cis-* and *trans*-epoxide, aldehyde, and ketone product-yields were calculated, as well as ketone and epoxide product-yield ratios for the addition of $O^3(P)$ to *cis-* and *trans*-2-butene, 2-pentene, 3-hexane, and 4-octene and *cis-* and *trans*-3,4-dimethyl-3-hexene (DMH) and 3-ethyl-2-methyl-2-pentene (MEP), respectively.

Results Information—Rule 3

(Step A) If you are writing an abstract of a document reporting on experimental research, tests, surveys, or case reports, reread the textual materials on the results or findings. While reading, condense this information mentally or write it on note paper, to aid your judgment of its relevance and significance.

Results information in sample paper A was discussed by the authors in paragraphs 2, 3, 5, and 6. An approximate version of the results of applying Step A of Rule 3 to two of these four paragraphs follows:

> [Paragraph 3] The *trans*-olefin compounds, as may be noted, produce epoxides that contain 90–97% of the *trans* form. . . .

Accordingly a ratio of 50:1 for the *trans*-epoxide/aldehyde compounds derived from the *trans* complex is obtained. . . . The *trans*-epoxide/ketone ratio obtained from the *cis*- as compared to the *trans*-olefin shows the largest difference with 4-octene. . . . The aldehyde/ketone ratio resulting from the *cis*-4-octene–oxygen complex is calculated to be about 7. [INDEX TERMS: *trans*-olefins produced trans-epoxides; differences in *trans*-epoxide/aldehyde ratios and *trans*-epoxide/ketone ratios]

[Paragraph 5] The O(^{3}P) reaction gives, in addition to 3,4-epoxy-3,4-dimethylhexane, two ketones, namely, 4,4-dimethyl-3-hexanone and 3-ethyl-3-methyl-2-pentanone, depending on whether the methyl or ethyl group migrates. The reaction gives no other products. . . . The same two ketones are produced from MEP as from *cis*- and trans-DMH. . . . Ketone II results from ethyl migration starting with DMH, or methyl migration starting with MEP. [INDEX TERMS: oxygen addition to DMH produces 3,4-epoxy-3,4-dimethylhexane and two ketones; ketone II results from ethyl or methyl migration]

Step B of rule 3 specifies: *Extract the most relevant results and write them in sentence form, concisely, in descending order of significance.* The results information reported in the abstract also should be consistent with the information on purpose, scope, and methods given in the first part of the abstract. Suggested results sentences for sample abstract A are:

Comparison of the *trans*-epoxide to ketone ratios from the *cis*- vs. the *trans*-olefin indicates that these ratios diverged with increasing size of the olefin. Reactions of larger olefins were more stereospecific; *cis*-3-hexene gave about 2.5 times as much *cis*-3,4-epoxyhexane as the *trans*-epoxide. *Trans*-olefin compounds produced epoxides containing 90–97% of the *trans* form, resulting in a 50:1 ratio for the *trans*-epoxide/aldehyde compounds from the *trans* complex. The *trans*-epoxide/ketone ratio obtained from the *cis*- as compared to the *trans*-olefin showed the largest difference with 4-octene. Besides 3,4-epoxy-3,4-dimethyl hexane, oxygen addition using DMH gave 4,4-dimethyl-3-hexanone (I) and 3-ethyl-3-methyl-2-pentanone (II) ketones, depending on whether the methyl or ethyl group migrated. The reaction gave no other products. Using MEP the same two ketones were produced as from *cis*- and *trans*-DMH; but ketone (I) resulted from methyl and ethyl group migration, starting with DMH and MEP, respectively. Opposite migrations produced ketone II.

Conclusions Information—Rule 4

(Step A) Reread the conclusions and recommendations that were identified during the retrieval-reading process in a manner similar to that described in Rule 3.

(Step B) Extract the most relevant conclusions and recommendations and write them in sentence form, tersely, in descending order of significance.

The final sentences in sample abstract A will contain conclusions information only. No recommendations information was presented in the sample paper. The authors did present a significant amount of discussion in seven paragraphs of the paper on their conclusions based on the research findings. The following seven sentences were extracted and modified for the abstract from two of these paragraphs (paragraphs 4 and 8). Appendix 5 contains illustrations of the creative reading-through-indexing process for all seven of the paragraphs.

Results suggest that retention of configuration of products is dependent on olefin chain length, and that reaction of oxygen atoms at low temperature is more stereospecific with *trans*-olefins. Stereotransformation of the transition intermediate requires a 180° rotation of one of the carbon atoms of the double bond with its attached groups about the modified olefinic bond, which occurs with the *cis*-olefins. Stereotransformation is a factor of rates of ring closure and rearrangement leading to final products, compared to the *cis–trans* interchange in the complex. Ring closure probably is independent of olefin size. Concerted rearrangement involving oxygen localization and group migration requires electronic and spatial reorganization. Addition of ground-state, triplet oxygen to singlet-state olefin to give singlet-state products probably requires a relaxation process. Group migration probably involves a transient bridging of the bond carbon pair, and intermediate relaxation to final products could involve steric effects.

Provisional abstracting of sample paper A is now complete. The abstract was purposefully made lengthier than is normal for a paper of the type and length of the sample one. This was done to demonstrate amply the kinds of information that have potential for inclusion in the abstract and, subsequently, to show how the size can be reduced by applying the rules for critical reading for the self-editing of abstracts. The application of the rules is described in Chapter 12.

Chapter 10

Creative Reading for Sample Abstract B

There are twenty critical minutes in the evolution of my paintings. The closer I get to that time—those twenty minutes—the more intensively subjective I become—but the more objective, too. Your eyes gets sharper: you become continuously more critical.

—Philip Guston

Time Required to Write Abstracts

Little is written in the recent literature on how long it takes an access abstractor to write an abstract. This is probably a consequence of the difficulties in measuring or estimating the time needed.

One of the measurement problems stems from the fact that access abstractors, working on the staffs at information system facilities or free-lance, may write original abstracts on simple or complex themes, edit or modify author abstracts, or write translation abstracts. Each task has its own range of time requirements. Usually, the information in the materials to be abstracted is presented concisely and in a unified manner, and the information on purpose, scope, methods, findings, and conclusions can be located with little difficulty. Occasionally, however, the information is written incoherently or ambiguously, or is poorly organized, and extra time and effort are required during the retrieval- and creative-reading processes for abstracting.

Nevertheless, the 20-minute spell of creativity that was discussed by the late American artist Philip Guston does serve well as an approximate figure for gauging the time that it should take a highly proficient access abstractor to write an original abstract of a difficult paper. Novice abstractors could take twice that time or longer. By original abstracts, I mean those for which the abstractor is instructed to concentrate on the materials in the body of the document while ignoring completely the author's abstract, if one is present, and preferably the author's title as well. The same proficient abstractor might take only about 12 minutes to write an abstract for a short, uncomplicated paper or monograph. The 12 to 20 minutes would be spent roughly as follows:

retrieval reading	3 to 5 minutes
creative reading	8 to 12 minutes
critical reading	1 to 3 minutes

After spending 12 to 20 minutes writing an abstract, the abstractor should take a short time-out of 3 to 5 minutes' duration. The exact length of the time-out is dependent on whether the abstractor will next write another original abstract or will do the less difficult task of modifying or editing an author's abstract.

For abstracting services that require the abstractor to catalog bibliographic data or to record index terms, an additional 5 to 10 minutes of processing time is required for each abstract. The cataloging of bibliographic data or recording of index terms by the abstractor is recommended only for low-volume abstracting projects. For moderate- and high-volume abstracting projects, abstractors should write only the abstracts. For cost- and quality-control effectiveness, bibliographic data and index terms should be entered by bibliographers and indexers, respectively. This contributes to higher productivity and greater accuracy and consistency by abstractors, indexers, and bibliographers alike.

Creative Reading of Sample Paper B—Primary Annotation

The rules for creative reading will now be applied to the writing of indicative and informative versions of sample abstract B. Step A of Rule 1 stipulates: *Reread all of the information on purpose, scope, and methods that you identified during the retrieval-reading process. While reading, mentally index the primary and secondary themes described in this material, using your own choice of arbitrary terms or phrases. (Beginning abstractors or those writing an abstract for a complex document might find it helpful to jot down their arbitrary index terms or phrases on note paper.)*

Sample paper B is a review of a book. Information on the purpose and scope of the book is contained in twelve of the paragraphs in the paper. Extracts of two of these paragraphs are shown below with arbitrary index terms. A complete version of the creative reading and arbitrary indexing for this paper is presented in Appendix 6.

[Paragraph 1] Jay W. Forrester's *Urban Dynamics* (M.I.T. Press) stands out in all this verbiage. The book has attracted attention because of the unorthodoxy of Forrester's recommendations, the self-assured manner in which he presents them, and his prominent use of the prestigious tools of systems analysis. With so many insistent voices saying that cities need more financial help from state and federal government, readers are likely to be impressed with Forrester's conclusion that help from the outside may "worsen conditions" in cities. Forrester, moreover, makes it difficult for readers to argue with him. With its appearance of rigor and scientism, its charts and diagrams, its arrays of numbers printed out by a computer, *Urban Dynamics* is rather intimidating. [INDEX TERMS: book review; systems analysis; urban dynamics]

[Paragraph 12] The supply of vacant land is a critical variable in Forrester's urban model. When more than half the land is still vacant, using additional land produces increasingly favorable effects. But once half the land in the city has been put to use—which in the simulations occurs at about 100 years—further depletions produce increasingly adverse effects. The city's growth is retarded, and stagnation and decline begin. As more land is used up, the scarcity of vacant land slows formation of new enterprises and construction of premium and worker housing, and speeds obsolescence of both enterprises and housing. [INDEX TERMS: land use; urban growth/decline; housing; industry]

Once the abstractor has rapidly reread and created a mental or written index of the annotative information in the article, the primary annotative or first sentence can be written in accordance with Step B of Rule 1. A suggested version follows.

The use of systems-analysis techniques and computer modeling as described by Jay W. Forrester in his book *Urban Dynamics* is evaluated.

Rule 2 may now be applied to complete the annotative information in the abstract. The following two sentences describe the scope of the remaining purpose information.

The interrelationships of public policy and financing, taxes, municipal expenditures, employment, housing, and population mobility are discussed. The effects of land supply and use also are considered.

Sample Paper B—Conclusions/Recommendations

If an indicative abstract was all that was required for this article, the creative reading for the writing of the abstract would be completed. The next step would be to begin the critical-reading or self-editing process. For purposes of illustrating the creative-reading process further, however, the abstract can be transformed into an informative one by applying Rule 4 on creative reading for writing information on conclusions and recommendations. (Rule 3 on the writing of information on results does not apply to sample paper B, since it is a book review.)

Seven of the fourteen paragraphs in the paper contain information on the conclusions and recommendations of the book reviewer. The results of creative reading for one of these paragraphs are shown below. The results of creative reading of the other paragraphs are illustrated in Appendix 6.

[Paragraph 1] . . . With its appearance of rigor and scientism, its charts and diagrams, its arrays of numbers printed out by a computer, *Urban Dynamics* is rather intimidating. [INDEX TERMS: intimidating use of charts, diagrams, and computer data]

After rapidly rereading all of the paragraphs containing conclusions and recommendations information, the informative portion of the abstract may be written in accordance with Step B of Rule 4. A suggested version follows.

The reviewer concludes that many of the urban management policies proposed in *Urban Dynamics* are inadequate or unrealistic. The significance of taxes and pragmatic financing of urban-renewal programs is overemphasized, and the cost of demolishing low-income housing and the potential for using vacant lands beyond city limits are overlooked. No explicit mention is made in Forrester's systems analysis of reciprocal urban and suburban effects. Responsibilities and functions of local governments should be redistributed to avoid pursuance of narrow self-interests. The reviewer recommends that funding from non-local sources should be used to reduce municipal taxes rather than to increase municipal expenditures.

The provisional writing of a full informative abstract for sample article B is now complete. Self-editing of the abstract through critical reading is described in Chapter 13.

PART IV

CRITICAL READING
AND RULES

INDICATIVE ABSTRACT:

Critical-reading techniques for the self-editing of abstracts by authors and access abstractors are described. Rules for critical reading are used in the editing of two sample abstracts. The function of thinking and cognition skills within abstracting and other information-processing activities is discussed. A syntopical index to the literature on abstracting style and additional examples of abstracts are presented.

Chapter 11

Critical Reading for Abstracting

The abstractor should develop the practice of critically rereading the completed abstract and should chop ruthlessly at all verbiage before forwarding it to the reviewer.

—GUIDE TO ABSTRACTING AND INDEXING
FOR NUCLEAR SCIENCE ABSTRACTS

The creative reading discussed in Part II is done to record rapidly on paper in the required format, both coherently and concisely, the most relevant information from the material being abstracted. Rules and conventions for abstracting are important during this process but are not the primary concern. They should not interfere with the smooth flow of writing. However, rules and conventions for writing good idiomatic English become a primary concern during the critical-reading stage of analytical reading for abstracting. The form and content also continue to be a concern during critical reading.

Critical reading usually should take 1 to 3 minutes, depending on the length and complexity of the abstract and the reading skill of the abstractor.

Benefits of Critical Reading

Critical reading, the first quality check of the abstract, is helpful for catching errors at the source. The act of critical reading reinforces the abstractor's understanding of the rules for abstracting. By screening out errors in style and content at the source, the abstractor allows reviewers and editors to be more productive while they are further refining the quality of the abstract. Critical reading is also beneficial as a way of identifying questions or problems of style that either may be resolved independently by the abstractor or may be brought to the attention of the editor or reviewer. Rules for critical reading are given in the next chapter.

Syntopical Index for Critical Reading

Each primary or secondary publisher or distributor of abstracts has special rules and instructions for the style and content of abstracts. For small abstracting services, these might fit on a single page of paper; for larger ones, they might fill a full-size instruction manual. Besides the instruction sheets or manuals, some abstracting services maintain a collection of general style guidelines for writing. Many professional abstractors maintain their own collection of abstracting instructions and writing guidebooks. Others find that use of a good, comprehensive dictionary solves most of their problems adequately.

As an editor and trainer of abstractors, I have accumulated many writing aids for abstracting. The research done for preparation of this book has at least doubled the size of my collection. From it I have compiled indexes on abstracting aids and points of style. I suggest that abstractors and editors use these indexes to augment their present collection or as starter indexes if they don't yet have a collection. The first index, presented in Figure 7, was compiled from sources devoted specifically to abstracting. It is labeled as "syntopical" because it includes extracts on points of style taken from the literature cited. The second index, presented in Appendix 7, is based on more general writing and editing manuals and contains headings and citations to pages only.

FIG. 7. *Syntopical index to the literature on abstracting style. In the citations presented the number preceding the colon represents one of the following six references; the numbers following the colon represent pages in the reference cited. The extracts are from the reference indicated in parentheses.*

1. American National Standards Institute, Inc. *American National Standard for Writing Abstracts.* ANSI Z39.14-1979. American National Standards Institute, Inc., New York, 1979
2. Borko, H., and C. L. Bernier. *Abstracting Concepts and Methods.* Academic Press, New York, 1975
3. Borko, H., and S. Chatman. Criteria for acceptable abstracts: a survey of abstractors' instructions. *American Documentation* 14(2):149–160, 1963
4. Collison, R. *Abstracts and abstracting services.* Clio Press, Santa Barbara, Calif., 1971
5. Maizell, R. E., J. F. Smith, and T. E. R. Singer. *Abstracting Scientific and Technical Literature; an Introductory Guide and Text for Scientists, Abstractors, and Management.* Wiley-Interscience, New York, 1971
6. Weil, B. H., I. Zarember, and H. Owen. Technical-abstracting fundamentals. II. Writing principles and practices. *Journal of Chemical Documentation* 3(2):125–132, 1963

Style point:	*Citation:*	*Extract:*
Abbreviations	2:10–11 6:129	Ad hoc abbreviations may be used by abstractors for long words repeated several times in an abstract. Such abbreviations are given in parentheses after the first occurrence of the name in full and are thereafter used consistently throughout the abstract.[2]

		Use standard abbreviations for physical units and commonplace words. Heavy use of abbreviations is an obvious way of shortening an abstract, but it is one that slows reading considerably.[6]
Accuracy	1:9 2:11–12 5:210	Reducing the number of errors to the barest minimum is a necessary, although expensive, goal of the abstracting service. . . . Omissions are the most serious kind of error, for the user cannot be expected to detect what isn't there. Content errors can be reduced in number by instructing and training the abstractor. Feedback is essential, as is editorial alertness.[2]
Ambiguity (*see* Clarity)		
Articles	6:130	Avoid both overusing and awkward omission of articles, e.g., "Pressure is a function of temperature," not "The pressure is a function of the temperature," but "The refinery operated. . . ," not "Refinery operated . . ."[6]
Brevity	2:9–11 2:68–70 4:13 5:78	All natural languages, such as English, are full of redundancy, much of which can be eliminated during abstracting of the original document. Abstract users read abstracts knowing that they must be alert to every word, and they must, in places, read in reasonable surmises. . . . Descriptions of well-known techniques, equipment, processes, conclusions, premises, axioms, and results—common knowledge, what one educated or trained in the fields is expected to know—are commonly omitted from abstracts. . . . Only what the author has done and the results are abstracted. What the investigator tried to do but did not accomplish, and what he intends to do next, while perhaps important in the original article, are generally omitted from the abstract as a matter of policy.[2]

Users with ready access to strong libraries may require less lengthy abstracts.[5] |
Clarity	2:13 5:210	The abstract is clear and unambiguous. Trade names, jargon, acronyms, and the like are either adequately explained or not used at all.[5]
Colloquialisms	6:130	Use trade jargon and colloquialisms sparingly and carefully. Although jargon can give an authentic flavor to an abstract, its use has pitfalls. The same jargon words may mean different things in different fields, or nothing at all except to a very few readers.[6]
Conciseness	2:21–24 5:80–81	He (the abstractor) does not waste words. He avoids repetitive and meaningless expressions. He knows that superlatives and other adjectives are not usually necessary.[5]

FIG. 7. *Continued*

Consistency	4:52–53 5:6	An abstractor cannot be expected to cover everything thoroughly—to do so would defeat the purpose of the abstract. Also, most abstractors write in a way that reflects their training, experience, and interests, no matter how objective they try to be. Users should know about this "built-in" limitation of abstracts.[5]
Extracting	2:21 2:162–163 5:77	The abstractor can attempt to paraphrase in concise form what the author of the original document has said. But he will often want to retain as much as possible of the original emphasis and terminology for the sake of accuracy. He may want to use brief direct excerpts to prevent changing meanings because of any subjective leanings he may have or because of excessive zeal for compactness.[5]
Jargon (*see* Clarity, Colloquialisms)		
Length (*see* Brevity)		
Paraphrasing (*see* Extracting)		
Point of view	3:18	There is often a close correlation between one's notion of the function of abstracts and his rhetorical point of view; in informative abstracts, the abstractor will be completely identified with the author, while in descriptive abstracts, the abstractor will stand apart, behind locutions like "X was attempted" or "The author believes Y."[3]
Punctuation	2:74	Punctuation in abstracts is the same as in any good prose form. . . . Complete sentences and abbreviations (except those of units of measurement) have periods. Commas are used to separate members of a series, and a comma is placed just before the conjunction connecting the last two members of a series. Semicolons are used for combining closely related sentences into one sentence and for separating parts of series in which commas are used within one or more of the parts.[2]
Redundancy	2:9–10	All natural languages, such as English, are full of redundancy, much of which can be eliminated during abstracting of the original document. Abstract users read abstracts knowing that they must be alert to every word, and they must, in places, read in reasonable surmises.[2]
Symbols (*see* Abbreviations)		
Synonyms	6:130	Avoid the overuse of synonyms that can lead to absurd-sounding phrases—the so-called "sin of syn-

FIG. 7. *Continued*

onyms." We would not say: "The resin exchanges potassium ions for *basic electrolytes.*" We would simply be content with ". . . hydroxyl ions," despite the repetition of "ions."[6]

Telegraphic writing	2:74 3:15 5:81 5:121	A telegraphic style is undesirable. A few beginning abstractors may write this way in the hope of saving space. Complete sentences and only authorized abbreviations should be used.[2]
Terseness (*see* Conciseness)		
Verb tense	3:17 6:129	The past tense is used in describing experimental work, including the procedure, equipment, conditions, theoretical bases, and data obtained. The present tense is used in giving conclusions derived from the experimental data.[3]
Voice	1:10 3:16 6:129	Use verbs in the active voice whenever possible; they contribute to clear, brief, forceful writing. However, the passive voice may be used for indicative statements and even for informative statements in which the receiver of the action should be stressed.[1]

Fig. 7. *Continued*

Chapter 12

Critical Reading for Sample Abstract A

. . . And so
I say unto you: beware the right margin
Which is unjustified; the left
Is justified and can take care of itself
But what is in between expands and flaps . . .
— JOHN ASHBERRY

Creative-reading versions of sample abstracts A and B were written and discussed in Chapters 9 and 10. The abstracts are probably longer, if not better, versions than ones that might have been written routinely by author or access abstractors, because extra time and effort were put into writing them, to make them good illustrations. Nevertheless, there is still much that can be done to improve the style and content of these abstracts. Partially true to the warning in Ashberry's poem, although the right margins are justified, in between the margins there are definitely some overexpanded extracts from the text of the sample articles and sentences that contain words and phrases that ambiguously flap out of sequence or out of context. However, these samples can be made into best-quality abstracts by applying the rules of critical reading which will take care of the tucking in and smoothing out of the editorial flaps that were introduced during the creative-reading phase.

Rules for Critical Reading

There are three rules for the self-editing of completed abstracts by use of critical reading. Experienced abstractors should have no difficulty applying the rules simultaneously during a single analytical reading of the text of most of their abstracts. Novice abstractors are advised to follow the rules separately in sequence. The rules are interrogatory.

Rule 1. Is the abstract properly structured and unified?
Rule 2. Is the content of the abstract complete, coherent, and concise?

Rule 3. Does the abstract conform to both general style rules and conventions for abstracts and those special ones contained in the publisher's or information-system manager's instructions on the type and length of abstracts?

Critical Reading for Sample Abstract A

Sample or provisional abstract A conforms well with the requirements of critical-reading rules 1 and 2, and partially with those of rule 3. It has good structure, and the information on purpose, methods, results, and conclusions is relatively unified. Whether or not sample abstract A conforms to rules on types of abstracts, it does violate at least one recommendation on the preferred length of abstracts. The *American National Standard for Writing Abstracts*[2] suggests that abstracts for most papers and portions of monographs be kept to fewer than 250 words. Provisional abstract A is well over 300 words long. The deletion of most of three of the sentences containing detailed information on results and three of the sentences that elaborate on the primary conclusions of the study will reduce the size of the abstract by over 100 words to a total that is much closer to the 250 words recommended in the standard. The original version of sample abstract A is shown below with the sentences selected for deletion underlined.

The effects of oxygen atom addition to olefins on epoxide configuration rearrangements and migration of hydrogen and methyl and ethyl groups were studied at 90°K by using gas-liquid paper chromatography. *Cis–trans* isomerism in straight-chain, internal olefins and resulting epoxide compounds was determined. *Cis*- and *trans*-epoxide, aldehyde, and ketone product-yields were calculated, as well as ketone and epoxide product-yield ratios for the addition of O(^{3}P) to *cis*- and *trans*-2-butene, 2-pentene, 3-hexane, and 4-octene and *cis*- and *trans*-3,4-dimethyl-3-hexene (DMH) and 3-ethyl-2-methyl-2-pentene (MEP), respectively. Comparison of the *trans*-epoxide to ketone ratios from the *cis*- vs. the *trans*-olefin indicates that these ratios diverged with increasing size of the olefin. Reactions of larger olefins were more stereospecific; *cis*-3-hexene gave about 2.5 times as much *cis*-3,4-epoxyhexane as the trans-epoxide. *Trans*-olefin compounds produced epoxides containing 90–97% of the *trans* form, resulting in a 50:1 ratio for the *trans*-epoxide/aldehyde compounds from the *trans* complex. The *trans*-epoxide/ketone ratio obtained from the *cis*- as compared to the *trans*-olefin showed the largest difference with 4-octene. Besides 3,4-epoxy-3,4-dimethylhexane, oxygen addition using DMH gave 4,4-dimethyl-3-hexanone (I) and 3-ethyl-3-methyl-2-pentanone (II) ketones, depending on whether the methyl or ethyl group migrated. The reaction gave no other products. Using MEP, the same two ketones were produced as from *cis*- and *trans*-DMH; but ketone (I) resulted from methyl and ethyl group migration, starting with DMH and MEP, respectively. Opposite migrations produced ketone II. Results suggest that retention of configuration of products is dependent on olefin chain length and that reaction of oxygen atoms at low temperature is more stereospecific with *trans*-olefins. Stereotransformation of the transition intermediate requires a 180° rotation of one of the carbon atoms of the double bond with its attached groups about the modified olefinic bond, which occurs with the *cis*-olefins. Stereotransformation is a factor of rates of ring closure and rearrangement leading to final products, compared to the *cis-trans* interchange in the complex. Ring closure probably is independent of olefin size. Concerted rearrangement involving oxygen localization and group migration requires electronic and spatial reorganization. Addition of ground-state, triplet oxygen to singlet-state olefin to give singlet-state products probably requires a relaxation process. Group migration probably involves a transient bridging of the bond carbon pair, and intermediate relaxation to final products could involve steric effects.

The revised shorter version of sample abstract A follows.

The effects of oxygen atom addition to olefins on epoxide configuration rearrangements and migration of hydrogen and methyl and ethyl groups were studied at 90°K by using gas-liquid paper chromatography. *Cis-trans* isomerism in straight-chain, internal olefins and resulting epoxide compounds was determined. *Cis*- and *trans*-epoxide, aldehyde, and ketone product yields were calculated, as well as ketone and epoxide product-yield ratios for the addition of O(^{3}P) to *cis*- and *trans*-2-butene, 2-pentene, 3-hexane, and 4-octene and *cis*- and *trans*-3,4-dimethyl-3-hexene (DMH) and 3-ethyl-2-methyl-2-pentene (MEP), respectively. Comparison of the *trans*-epoxide to ketone ratios from the *cis*- vs. the *trans*-olefin indicates that these ratios diverged with increasing size of the olefin. Reactions of larger olefins were more sterospecific. Besides 3,4-epoxy-3,4-dimethylhexane, oxygen addition using DMH gave 4,4-dimethyl-3-hexanone (I) and 3-ethyl-3-methyl-2-pentanone (II) ketones, depending on whether the methyl or ethyl group migrated. The reaction gave no other products. Using MEP, the same two ketones were produced as from *cis-* and *trans*-DMH; but ketone (I) resulted from methyl and ethyl group migration, starting with DMH and MEP, respectively. Opposite migrations produced ketone II. Results suggest that retention of configuration of products is dependent on olefin chain length and that reaction of oxygen atoms at low temperature is more stereospecific with *trans*-olefins. Concerted rearrangement involving oxygen localization and group migration requires electronic and spatial reorganization. Addition of ground-state, triplet oxygen to singlet-state olefin to give singlet-state products probably requires a relaxation process. Group migration probably involves a transient bridging of the bond carbon pair, and intermediate relaxation to final products could involve steric effects.

Author Abstract of Sample Paper A

An author abstract was published with sample paper A and is shown in Figure 8. The author abstract is a good, informative one of about 100 words. It is written in findings-oriented format, which may be conventional for the journal in which it was published. With slight revisions it probably would be acceptable for inclusion in most access-information publications and data bases. A data base that includes the literature on chemical reactions at low temperature within its primary scope of coverage, however, would likely prefer to see more detailed information from this study in the abstract, such as that presented in sample abstract A.

Computer-Produced Abstract of Sample Paper A

Sample paper A also was abstracted as part of a dissertation research study by Mathis,[22] using a test automatic-abstracting system programmed

Rearrangements in the $O^3(P)$ atom addition to internal straight-chain olefins involve, as one of the processes, internal rotations resulting in configurational changes. Symmetrical *cis*-olefins at 90°K were found to show greater stereospecificity in the oxygen atom addition reaction as the chain length was increased. Rearrangements involving migration of alkyl groups and localization of oxygen on one of the carbon atoms of the olefinic pair occur in a concerted manner. This was shown from the reactions of 3-ethyl-2-methyl-2-pentene and two of its isomers. Clearly, independent rates cannot be associated with migrating alkyl groups, and additional factors, other than electron density, determine the position of addition of the oxygen atom.

FIG. 8. *Author abstract of sample paper A.*

for the IBM 370 computer. Called ADAM (Automatic Document Abstracting Method), the system was developed originally by J. E. Rush, M. Salvador, and A. Zamora at Ohio State University. Mathis introduced a modification to the ADAM system. Resembling the critical-reading stage of manual abstracting, the modification is designed to improve the form, arrangement, and content of the sentences selected for the abstract. The improved, computer-produced test abstract of sample paper A is shown in Figure 9. It contains 364 words, comprising 18 sentence-length extracts from the paper.

A consideration of the oxygen atom addition to *cis*- and *trans*-2-butene in the temperature region 77 to 113 K led to the formulation of a new transition intermediate. In this intermediate, the oxygen atom is represented as bound in a loose, three-membered ring with, and in the plane of, the olefinic structure of the reactant. Observations on 2-butenes have been extended to several more straight-chain, internal olefins in the low-temperature region. Comparison of the *trans*-epoxide to ketone ratios from the *cis*- vs. the *trans*-olefin with increasing size of the olefin indicates that these ratios diverge. Reaction of oxygen atoms in the low-temperature region tends to be more stereospecific with *trans*- than with *cis*-olefins. Carbonyl compounds constitute a sizeable fraction of the products of the oxygen atom addition to olefins in the low-temperature region and, as has been noted, an intramolecular group migration is required for carbonyl formation. The principal carbonyl product in the *trans*-2-butene reaction at 90 K is 2-butanone. The formation of this ketone requires the migration of H. Compared to the migration of the methyl group, that of H is slightly favored. *cis*-2-Butene is not useful for the comparison, as both of the hydrogen atoms attached to the olefinic carbon pair are suppressed through interaction with oxygen in the complex. The relative quantities of 2-butanone to isobutyraldehyde are taken as a measure of the ratio of migration of the hydrogen atom to the methyl group. Reactions were effected at 90 K in the apparatus routinely used for this purpose. The olefins were diluted 10 to 1 with propane. The exposure time of oxygen atoms was 5 minutes, and about 1% of the olefin was reacted. The products were determined at 135 K and a helium flow of 100 cc/minute. The *cis* and *trans* isomers of 3,4-epoxy-3,4-dimethylhexane were not separable. Localization of the oxygen atom in the transition complex preceding alkyl group rearrangement is not in accord with the experimental results. At 90 K, the ratio of addition to C-2 is 16 times that to C-3. For MEP, addition of the oxygen atom to that carbon atom of the double bond to which the two methyl groups are attached would be expected to be favored.

FIG. 9. *Improved computer-produced abstract of sample paper A.*

Chapter 13

Critical Reading for Sample Abstract B

Hints for Writing Good Reader-Oriented Informative Abstracts

Do:

scan the document purposefully for
   key facts

slant the abstract to your audience

tell what was found

tell why the work was done

tell how the work was done

place findings early in the topical
   sentence

put details in succeeding sentences

place general statements last

separate relatively independent
   subjects

differentiate experiment from
   hypothesis

be informative but brief

be exact, concise, and unambiguous

use short, complete sentences

Don't:

change the meaning of the original

comment on or interpret the
   document

mention earlier work

include detailed experimental results

describe details for conventional
   apparatus

mention future work

begin abstracts with stock phrases

use involved phraseology

use questionable jargon

waste words by stating the obvious

say the same thing two ways

use noun form of verbs

over-use synonyms

use a choppy, telegraphic style

The above *do*'s and *don't*'s for reader-oriented abstracts, which were compiled by Weil et al.,[35] are presented here to show one more good example of the rules of abstracting. Most of their rules are also applicable to the writing of the purpose-oriented abstracts discussed in this book. In fact, reiterating what I have said, development and use of good analytical-reading and thinking skills, in combination with acceptable writing and

73

editing skills that are amenable to improvement, and adherence to rules and conventions for abstracting, should enable most individuals to become good abstractors no matter what type of abstract is called for.

Critical Reading for Sample Abstract B

The three rules for critical reading will now be applied to the sample abstract of the book review, which was originally published in *Fortune*. First, I will reproduce the provisional version of sample abstract B from Chapter 10:

> The use of systems-analysis techniques and computer modeling as described by Jay W. Forrester in his book *Urban Dynamics* is evaluated. The interrelationships of public policy and financing, taxes, municipal expenditures, employment, housing, and pop-
> 5 ulation mobility are discussed. The effects of land supply and use are also considered. The reviewer concludes that many of the urban management policies proposed in *Urban Dynamics* are inadequate or unrealistic. The significance of taxes and prag-matic financing of urban renewal programs is overemphasized,
> 10 and the cost of demolishing low-income housing and the potential for using vacant lands beyond city limits are overlooked. No explicit mention is made in Forrester's systems analysis of recip-rocal urban and suburban effects. Responsibilities and functions of local governments should be redistributed to avoid pursuance
> 15 of narrow self-interests. The reviewer recommends that funding from non-local sources should be used to reduce municipal taxes rather than to increase municipal expenditures.

Is this abstract properly structured and unified in accordance with Rule 1 of critical reading for abstracting? No, it is not. The next to the last sentence, which begins on line 13 with the word "Responsibilities," is presented as the last in a series of conclusion sentences. It is, in fact, a recommendations sentence and it should be relocated after the conclu-sions.

Is this abstract complete, coherent, and concise? Hardly. There is much room for improvement through further critical self-editing. Recasting of the sentence that begins on line 11 with the words "No explicit" would make for smoother reading. There is always room for improving concise-ness. At least one needless word can be eliminated from each sentence. The elimination process and the other editing changes are shown below by use of editing symbols:

The use of systems-analysis techniques and computer modeling as ~~described by~~ *proposed in* Jay W. Forrester, ~~in his book~~ *Urban Dynamics* is evaluated. The interrelationships of public policy and financing, taxes, municipal expenditures, employment, housing, ~~and~~ population mobility, ~~are discussed. The effects of~~ *and* land supply and use are ~~also~~ considered. The reviewer concludes that many of the urban management policies proposed ~~in Urban Dynamics~~ are inadequate or unrealistic; ~~The significance of~~ tax *ation* and pragmatic financing of urban renewal programs ~~is~~ *are* overemphasized, and the cost of demolishing low-income housing and the potential for using vacant *rural* lands ~~beyond city limits~~ are overlooked. No explicit mention is made in Forrester's systems analysis of reciprocal urban and suburban effects. Responsibilities and functions of local governments should be redistributed to avoid ~~pursuance of narrow~~ *emphasizing* self-interests. The reviewer recommends that funding from non-local sources should be used to reduce municipal taxes rather than to increase municipal expenditures.

For the sake of brevity in the discussion at this point, I will assume that the resulting version of sample abstract B complies with all three rules of critical reading for the self-editing of abstracts:

The use of systems-analysis techniques and computer modeling as proposed in Jay W. Forrester's *Urban Dynamics* is evaluated. The interrelationships of public policy and financing, taxes, municipal expenditures, employment, housing, population mobility, and land supply and use are considered. The reviewer concludes that many of the urban management policies proposed are inadequate or unrealistic; taxation and pragmatic financing of urban renewal programs are overemphasized, and the cost of demolishing low-income housing and the potential for using vacant rural lands are overlooked. No explicit mention of reciprocal urban and suburban effects is made in Forrester's analysis. The reviewer recommends that funding from non-local sources should be used to reduce municipal taxes rather than to increase municipal expenditures. Responsibilities and functions of local governments should be redistributed to avoid emphasizing self-interests.

Computer-Produced Abstract of Sample Paper B

Sample paper B was also abstracted by the ADAM test automatic-abstracting system, but not improved by using the Mathis modification. For comparison with sample abstract B, this abstract is shown in Figure 10. It contains 244 words; all of which were extracted from two of the fifteen paragraphs in the sample paper (paragraphs 2 and 7).

Forrester, A professor at M.I.T.'s Sloan School of Management, relies on a computer model he developed to simulate the growth, decline, and stagnation of a hypothetical city from birth to old age (250 years). Such methods have a great deal of potential for the analysis of urban problems and have already demonstrated their value in a number of specific, though limited applications. However, the development of truly useful and trustworthy urban simulation models remains a distant objective and will require much greater resources than have yet been devoted to the task. Before adequate models become available, many inadequate ones will be put forward. Forrester's model is a conspicuous example. In his first chapter Forrester warns the reader that caution should be exercised in applying the model to actual situations. Subsequently, however, he expresses few reservations about the model's validity and freely uses it as a basis for prescribing public policy. The influence of tax rates on employment and population structure in Forrester's city is powerful and pervasive. "Managerial-professional" and "labor" families are assumed to be repelled by high tax rates, whereas the underemployed are indifferent to them. High tax rates, moreover, discourage the formation of new enterprises and accelerate the aging of existing ones. There are still other adverse effects: high taxes retard construction of both premium and worker housing, which in turn discourages the kinds of people who live in these kinds of housing from moving into the city or remaining there.

FIG. 10. *Computer-produced abstract of sample paper B.*

Chapter 14

Thinking, Cognition, and Abstracting

> Thinking on THINKING
> Patterns of THINKING and Writing
> The Art of Clear THINKING
> Clear THINKING and its Relationship to
> Clear Writing
> Scientific THINKING and Scientific Writing
> Sounder THINKING Through Clearer Writing
> THINKING Straight: Principles of
> Reasoning for Readers and Writers

Most of the titles of monographs and articles shown above are cited in the permuted index to *An Annotated Bibliography on Technical Writing, Editing, Graphics, and Publishing: 1950–1965*.[25] One of these titles, Pacifico's "Thinking on Thinking," is to a series of four articles in *Chem-Tech*.[24] In these articles, Pacifico offers a broad-ranging "guided tour of the thinking process" that is aimed at "minimizing erroneous thinking by characterizing correct thinking." As is evident in the titles of the other works cited in the permuted index, their authors are concerned primarily with thinking in relation to writing.

Critical Thinking and Reading

Besides dealing with the relationship between thinking and writing, Beardsley, in his book *Thinking Straight: Principles of Reasoning for Readers and Writers*,[5] is also concerned about thinking and reading. In a "Preview" to the body of his text, he describes thinking as a "series of ideas that is directed toward the solution of a problem." Further in his discussion of problem solving, Beardsley uses words that implicitly relate to the kind of thinking that is done during the problem solving associated with the abstracting of texts. Problem solving, he notes, "takes imagina-

77

tion, sensitivity, persistence, concentration, the ability to obtain and connect much *relevant information* [italics added]. But without some skill in logic, the task is hopeless."

The second half of Beardsley's book is on the theme of language and critical thinking. Essentially, the steps that abstractors take in reading materials analytically while thinking logically and rigorously are excellent mental-training activities for acquiring proficiency in critical thinking.

The term ABSTRACTING as such is not one of the headings in the subject index at the close of Beardsley's book, but a careful reading of his work would complement the knowledge abstractors gain by reading other works that are more directly pertinent to abstracting.

Clearer Abstracts Through Sounder Thinking

In his article "Sounder Thinking Through Clearer Writing" [37] Woodford discusses the causes and effects of the inferior writing that is published in some scientific journals. This writing often results from "an inward confusion of thought." Exposure to it "exerts a corrupting influence on young scientists—on their writing, their reading, and their thinking." Woodford's experience in giving a course in scientific writing revealed that some of his students had been so "warped" by studying poor examples of writing in the scientific literature that their ability to write abstracts had been damaged.

> As one of the assignments in my course, my students had to write an abstract of a published paper. The paper itself was brief, simple, and well written. I was dismayed to find that at least half of my students misread the paper in three major ways. First, they referred to 20-day-old rats, although the age of the animals was never given—the article described 20-gram rats; second, they talked about specific activity of the cholesterol injected, whereas the specific activity was never stated—the figure they had got hold of was actually the number of millicuries injected per kilogram of rat body weight, and they had misread it as mc/mg; last, and most amazing of all, they gave conclusions directly opposite to those indicated both by the data and by the authors of the article they were abstracting!

Woodford recommends that students complete a graduate course on scientific writing to strengthen their scientific thinking. The course should concentrate on "logic, precision, and clarity; on how these qualities can be achieved in writing; and on how such achievement strengthens the corresponding faculties in thinking."

A few more specific hints on sounder thinking while writing clearer abstracts follow.

- A logical format for composing the abstract, preferably purpose- or findings-oriented, should be selected, and the required order for representing the relevant information should be adhered to.
- A judgment on what information is relevant for inclusion in the abstract should be suspended until the full text has been read.
- Multiple versions of the same relevant information in a text should be compared, and the most pertinent details should be consolidated for extraction into the abstract.
- Author abstractors should assign precise meanings to the words that they use in their abstracts. Access abstractors should attempt to substitute more precise words for any unclear or ambiguous ones that they extract from the material being abstracted. The substitutions should be made, however, *only* after the abstractors are convinced that there is not the slightest possibility that the author's meaning will be distorted in the process.
- The significance of certain relevant information should not be over-emphasized at the expense of other equally or more relevant information through careless or inadequate reading of the text of the basic document.
- Abstracts should be composed in such a way that no doubt is created in the reader's mind as to whether the results, conclusions, and recommendations presented therein are, in fact, the author's, rather than those of other researchers whose work the author has cited in the basic document.
- The size of purpose-oriented abstracts should not be inflated by ending them with statements on conclusions that were already implied in the results. For example, if an abstract of a study on the effects of sleep deprivation on human performance of information-processing tasks already contains specific details on negative effects, a concluding statement to the effect that "Sleep deprivation interferes with human performance of cognitive tasks" should not be added to it. Similarly, when findings-oriented abstracts are composed, the subject of the study need not be stated if it can be clearly perceived from the findings statements.
- All abstractors should persistently motivate themselves to use clear and sound thinking whether they are writing single abstracts as authors or large volumes of abstracts as access abstractors.

Cognition

The girl diner in the classic Carl Rose cartoon shown on the next page perceives in her mind that broccoli is much the same vegetable as spinach, which she has no desire to consume. A review of 15 volumes of *Infor-*

"*It's broccoli, dear.*"
"*I say it's spinach, and I say the hell with it.*"

Drawing by Carl Rose; © 1928, 1956
The New Yorker Magazine, Inc.

mation *Science Abstracts* and its predecessor publications indicates that
adult abstractors who desire to sample thoughts on the subject of
"thinking" in relation to information processing would find little that is
pertinent in the literature on information science, but they would find an
abundance of recent writings in this literature that could be indexed under
the related concept "cognition."

In his *Dictionary of Philosophy*,[3] Angeles defines the terms cognition
and thinking thusly:

> **cognition.** 1. Intellectual knowledge. 2. The act of knowing.
>
> **thinking.** 1. A mental activity whereby a person uses concepts ac-
> quired in the process of learning and directs them toward some goal
> and/or object. 2. Any of the mental activities of which we are
> conscious, such as reflecting, inferring, remembering, introspecting,
> retrospecting, doubting, willing, feeling, understanding, apprehend-
> ing, perceiving, meditating, imagining, pondering, etc.

If they wish to determine where their function of abstracting fits in the
total information-processing scheme, abstractors who use skills that they
acquired or refined through learning how to abstract while they analytically read the rapidly growing literature on the role of human cognition
in information processing should rely heavily during their reading on just
two of the fourteen mental activities associated with thinking that Angeles
cites. These two mental activities are "inferring" and "imagining." With
these activities uppermost in mind while reading, abstractors may thus
gain additional insights into ways of thinking more clearly while writing
or editing abstracts.

Cognition and Information Processing

A survey on the subject of cognition and information processing is
presented in the September and November 1981 issues of the *Journal of
the American Society for Information Science*.[14] Griffith,[13] in his introduction to the collection of articles comprising this survey, states that
information science must adapt or build an applied cognitive science if
information processing and handling are to be improved substantially.
The emphasis of the articles in this collection is on human problem-
solving behavior during information processing, and a wealth of material
on the topic of the use of the computer to simulate this behavior is
included.

In his article "The Organization and Use of Information: Contributions
of Information Science, Computational Linguistics and Artificial Intelligence," Walker[32] is concerned primarily with computer-based procedures

for information retrieval and with the processing of both information and knowledge. Within his analysis of the development and use of advanced information systems, abstractors would find materials that are most relevant to their own information-processing tasks in his discussion on "strategies for representing the information contained in a document."

Walker describes three forms of representation that are being investigated for use in the processing of text passages for three computer-based projects. The forms are "metatexts," "messages," and "annotations." The last term is reminiscent of Lancaster and Herner's earlier work[20] on techniques for human-based representation of texts through the use of modular abstracts containing representative combinations of annotations and informative, indicative, and critical abstracts.

Simon reviews advances since about 1972 in modeling human cognitive processes, particularly by computer simulation.[27] He discusses theories of these processes in terms of problem solving, semantic memory, induction of patterns, learning and development, and motivation and emotion. Within his broad theoretical analysis of information processing, the specialty of abstracting, or any of the other conventional specialties that fall within the scope of access services, are not mentioned specifically. However, the concepts that abstractors store in their long-term memories should serve as convenient frames of reference to assist them in deepening their comprehension of Simon's advanced ideas on information processing.

A few extracts from Simon's summary of progress made in computer-assisted problem solving, for example, can be related approximately to abstracting concepts:

Extract	*Concept*
a problem space that could be searched effectively for a solution	retrieval reading of text to identify relevant information
understanding of the kinds of knowledge the expert must have and how that knowledge is stored in long-term memory and evoked by perceptual cues when relevant	abstractor's knowledge and evocation of rules on reading, thinking, writing, and editing
semantically rich domains (that is, domains requiring extensive knowledge for solving problems)	abstracting

Cognitive Science

Smith, in the 1980 *Annual Review of Information Science and Technology*,[28] includes information on the new disciplines of cognitive science

Topics in cognitive psychology	Corresponding topics in AI
*1. Perception (including sensation and concept formation)	*1. Pattern recognition, naming, relevance extraction
*2. Thinking	*2. Deduction, pathfinding, heuristics
*3. Remembering	*3. Conversing, information retrieval, question-answering
*4. Language comprehension	*4. Parsing, semantic "understanding"
*5. Motor behavior	5. Touching, moving, "seeing" by robots
*6. Motivation by needs and goals	*6. Goal seeking, optimization, satisfying
*7. Learning	*7. Reweighting, induction, discovery, generalization, adding assertions

FIG. 11. *Parallels between cognitive psychology and artificial intelligence (AI). Reprinted from Encyclopedia of Computer Science and Technology, Volume 5, 1976, by courtesy of Marcel Dekker, Inc.*

and knowledge engineering in her review of progress made in applications of artificial intelligence in information systems. The review contains a comprehensive guide to the literature on the new disciplines and a reproduction of Kochen's[18] table showing parallels between cognitive psychology and artificial intelligence. The table is reproduced in Figure 11 to show that there is an almost equal amount of parallels between cognitive psychology/science, artificial intelligence, and the mental activities and motivations of abstracting. The parallels are indicated by adding an asterisk to the all-but-one topics that are relevant to abstracting and abstractors.

Select Annotated Bibliography on Thinking and Cognition

Readers who would like guidance to the literature on the subjects of thinking, cognition, and information processing explicitly, and abstracting implictly, are referred to the select annotated bibliography contained in Appendix 4.

Chapter 15

Assisted Invitations to Precomposed Abstracts

> *This book . . . offers not rules and exhortations but*
> assisted invitations *to students of composition to discover*
> what they are trying to do and thereby how to do it.
> —ANN E. BERTHOFF

Thus far, this book on abstracting *has* offered rules and exhortations on how to compose abstracts and assisted invitations to follow the process during the composition of two sample abstracts. Before presenting a few rules and exhortations in the final part of the book on developing and maintaining cooperative professional relationships among abstractors, editors, managers, and users of abstracts, I will now present additional, but less formal, assisted invitations to examine completed sample abstracts.

Sample Abstracts

In her introduction to *Forming, Thinking, Writing: the Composing Imagination*,[7] Berthoff observes that most teachers agree that "the fundamentals of composing have to be presented, analyzed, demonstrated over and over again." Accordingly, the six sample precomposed abstracts that follow are shown in three versions: unedited purpose-oriented form, edited version of this form, and a findings-oriented verison of the edited abstract. The unedited versions are analyzed briefly by use of a modification of Brusaw, Alred, and Oliu's "Checklist of the Writing Process,"[10] which is presented in Figure 12.

Sample 1. Informative abstract composed from a translated report on occupational health epidemiology.

a. Unedited purpose-oriented form. Key for suggested revisions to this unedited abstract: *, replace abstract words with concrete ones; †, check for appropriate word choice; ‡, achieve conciseness.

Observations on the *skin tumors** in workers exposed to coal tar in a charcoal briquette factory were reported. Six of 10 cases of *tar tumors*† occurred inside the factory and 4 occurred on the outside. *All of the skin tumors involved the face.*‡ The principal localizations, in decreasing order of incidence, were the nose (8 *localizations*‡), the eyelids (7 *localizations*‡), the lips (4 *localizations*‡), and the ears (2 *localizations*‡). *The tumors appeared after widely varying periods of exposure, ranging from 1 year to 43 years.*‡ The histologic variety of these tumors was independent of the duration of exposure. *In half the cases,** there were multiple tumors. Three major types of tumors revealed by histologic results were keratoacanthoma, papilloma, and epithelioma. *All these tumors were curable with the therapeutic methods now available: electrocoagulation and radiotherapy.*‡ *In comparing the delay in appearance of tumors as a function of job assign-*

Check for completeness
Check for accuracy
Check for unity and coherence
Achieve effective transition
Check for consistent point of view
Emphasize main ideas
Subordinate less important ideas
Check for clarity
Eliminate ambiguity
Check for appropriate word choice
Eliminate affectation and jargon
Replace abstract words with concrete words
Achieve conciseness
Make writing active (voice)
Change negative writing to positive writing
Check for parallel structure
Check sentence construction and achieve sentence variety
Eliminate awkwardness
Check for appropriate tone
Eliminate problems of grammar
Eliminate sentence faults
Check for agreement
Check for proper case
Check for clear reference of pronouns
Eliminate dangling modifiers and misplaced modifiers
Check for correct punctuation
Check for mechanics: spelling, abbreviations, capital letters, contractions, italics, numbers, symbols, syllabification
Check for correctness of format

FIG. 12. *Checklist of the abstracting process (revision). Based on "Checklist of the Writing Process (Revision)" in Brusaw et al.*[10]

ment, it was noted that the 5 patients showing tumors within the first 10 years of exposure were those most highly exposed to the coal tar.‡

b. *Edited version of the purpose-oriented abstract in 1a.*

Ten case reports are presented of facial skin tumors in workers in a charcoal briquette factory who were exposed to coal tar. Six of the incidences occurred in workers inside the factory, and four occurred in workers outside. Principal localizations of the tumors were the nose, eyelids, lips, and ears, with 8, 7, 4, and 2 localizations, respectively. The tumors appeared after periods of exposure of 1 to 43 years. The histologic characteristics of the three major types of tumors identified (keratoacanthoma, papilloma, and epithelioma) were not exposure related. Five of the workers had multiple tumors. Five workers who had tumors within the first 10 years of exposure were among those who were most highly exposed to the coal tar. All tumors responded to electrocoagulation and radiotherapy.

c. *Findings-oriented version of the abstract in 1b.*

Facial skin tumors were identified in 10 workers exposed to coal tar in a charcoal briquette factory. Six of the incidences occurred in workers inside the factory, and four occurred in workers outside. Principal localizations of the tumors were the nose, eyelids, lips, and ears, with 8, 7, 4, and 2 localizations, respectively. The tumors appeared after periods of exposure of 1 to 43 years. The histologic characteristics of the three major types of tumors identified (keratoacanthoma, papilloma, and epithelioma) were not exposure related. Five of the workers had multiple tumors. The five workers who had tumors within the first 10 years of exposure were among those who were most highly exposed to the coal tar. All tumors responded to electrocoagulation and radiotherapy.

Sample 2. Informative abstract composed from an article on drug abuse and personality.

a. *Unedited purpose-oriented form.* Key for suggested revisions to this unedited abstract: *, check for unity and coherence; †, check for appropriate word choice; ‡, achieve conciseness; §, check for clarity.

The *personality characteristics** of adolescent drug abusers were *studied in a comparison‡* of an adolescent drug-abusing group and *an adolescent nonabusing group*‡ from middle and upper middle *classes.*§ *The variable of sex was also studied.** The Minnesota Multiphasic Personality Inventory (MMPI) *was used to evaluate personalities.** *Results showed that there were certain personality characteristics which distinguished adolescent drug abusers from nonabusers.*‡ Drug abusers were more nonconforming, tended to reject social conventions, and lacked the ability to form satisfactory emotional relationships. *No difference*† was found between male and female users based on MMPI scales.

b. *Edited version of the purpose-oriented abstract in 2a.*

Personality characteristics and sex of adolescent drug-abusing and nonabusing groups from middle- and upper-middle-class families were compared. The Minnesota Multiphasic Personality Inventory (MMPI) was administered to the two groups. Drug abusers were more nonconforming, tended to reject social conventions, and failed to form satisfactory emotional relationships. The MMPI revealed no significant differences between male and female users.

c. *Findings-oriented version of the abstract in 2b.*

Drug abusers were more nonconforming than nonabusers, tended to reject social conventions, and failed to form satisfactory emotional relationships, according to results obtained with middle- and upper-middle-class adolescents administered the Minnesota Multiphasic Personality Inventory. No significant differences were found between male and female drug users.

Sample 3. Informative abstract composed from a study in psychosociology.

a. *Unedited purpose-oriented form.* Key for suggested revisions to this unedited abstract: *, check for unity and coherence; †, check for appropriate word choice; ‡, achieve conciseness; §, check for clarity.

The problems of the child without a family and the best methods of providing for the needs felt by this child from infancy onward‡ are discussed. *The needs are described as simple:** the child should be welcomed, loved, given a feeling of "belonging." *The best solution of the child's problem is early permanent adoption by one family.** *If this proves impossible,*‡ successive foster-home situations should be avoided. *Careful psychological ex-*

aminations and advice should be accorded the child§ when a change of environment from foster home to foster home, or from institution to institution, is required. *If the child has suffered from lack of the above, his troubles should be identified and treated quickly.*§ The child should be taught early to retain, regain, or develop self-esteem. He should *always*† have a sole advisor *who can help him make and decide on necessary changes*§ and who has his full confidence.

b.   *Edited version of purpose-oriented abstract in 3a.*

Rearing of family-less children from infancy to adulthood was studied. The child should be welcomed, loved, and given a feeling of belonging, preferably through early permanent adoption by one family. Placement in successive foster homes should be avoided. Psychological examinations and constructive advice should be given when children change foster homes or institutions. Problem children should be identified and treated quickly. Family-less children should be taught early to retain, regain, or develop self-esteem. A single advisor who can help the child to adjust and who has his complete confidence should be assigned.

c.   *Findings-oriented version of the abstract in 3b.*

Family-less children should be welcomed, loved, and given a feeling of belonging from infancy to adulthood, preferably through early permanent adoption by one family. Placement in successive foster homes should be avoided. Psychological examinations and constructive advice should be given when children change foster homes or institutions. Problem children should be identified and treated quickly. Family-less children should be taught early to retain, regain, or develop self-esteem. A single advisor who can help the child to adjust and who has his complete confidence should be assigned.

Sample 4.   Informative abstract from a translated epidemiological report on opthalmology.

a.   *Unedited purpose-oriented form.* Key for suggested revisions to this unedited abstract: *, eliminate awkwardness; †, check for appropriate word choice; ‡, achieve conciseness; §, check for clarity.

The occurrence of macular hemorrhages and macular *holes*† *in cases of*‡ degenerative myopia was studied in 2511 eyes in 1525 patients *with degenerative myopia*‡ in Kyoto, Japan. Of the total, 1551 were female and 960 were male eyes, *indicating a preference for females.*‡ The number of cases of degenerative myopia increased *in proportion as both age and degree of myopia increased.** Macular hemorrhage was observed *in 114 eyes of which females were 70 and males 44.** A high incidence of macular hemorrhage was observed in the young and in the elderly group *and was frequently observed in cases of degenerative myopia of low degree,*§ *suggesting that macular hemorrhage is a complication in the early stages of degenerative myopia.*‡ Macular holes were observed in 182 eyes, *147 of which were of females and only 35 eyes were of males.** Macular holes resulting in retinal detachment were found in 80 female eyes and 11 male eyes. The formation of macular holes was *rarely seen in the young group and its incidence increased in proportion to aging.*§

b. *Edited version of the purpose-oriented abstract in 4a.*

Macular hemorrhages and vacuoles in degenerative myopia were studied in 2511 eyes in 1525 patients in Kyoto, Japan. The sample comprised 1551 female and 960 male eyes. The number of cases of degenerative myopia increased in proportion to increased age and degree of myopia. Macular hemorrhages were observed in 70 female and 44 male eyes. A high incidence of macular hemorrhaging was observed in young and elderly patients and in cases of minor degenerative myopia. Macular vacuoles were observed in 147 female and 35 male eyes; vacuoles resulting in retinal detachment were found in 80 female and 11 male eyes. The incidence of macular vacuoles increased with age. The vacuoles were rarely seen in younger patients.

c. *Findings-oriented version of the abstract in 4b.*

Macular hemorrhages and vacuoles were more prevalent in female patients with degenerative myopia. In 1525 patients in Kyoto, Japan, the number of cases of degenerative myopia also increased in proportion to increased age and degree of myopia. Macular hemorrhages were observed in 70 female and 44 male eyes of the 1551 female and 960 male eyes in the sample. A high incidence of macular hemorrhaging was observed in young and elderly patients and in cases of minor degenerative myopia. Macular vacuoles were observed in 147 female and 35 male eyes; vacuoles resulting in retinal detachment were found in 80 female and 11 male eyes. The incidence of macular vacuoles increased with age; the vacuoles were rarely seen in younger patients.

Sample 5. Informative abstract composed from an environmental science study.

a.   Unedited purpose-oriented form. Key for suggested revisions to this unedited abstract: *, eliminate awkardness; †, check for appropriate word choice; ‡, achieve conciseness; §, check for clarity.

The sources of potentially hazardous elements contained in urban roadway†,‡ were studied. A 648-gram sample of urban roadway dust was subdivided according to particle size, density, and ferromagnetic susceptibility and was analyzed for trace elements. Lead and cadmium were extracted from each sample and determined by atomic absorption spectrophotometry. Thirty-three other elements were found in a subsample by instrumental neutron activation analysis. Different methods were used to calculate the sources, then, by summing the source factors over all the samples, to calculate the percentage contribution to the total sample of each source.‡,§ This conclusion was derived: 76 percent (p) soil, 5.0 p cement, 0.3 p salt, 1.5 p automobile-exhaust particles, 7.7 p iron, 7.2 p automobile tire-wear particles, and 2.3 p unaccounted for.‡§ Statistical analysis was used to come to these conclusions, but the author suggests more detailed graphical presentation and more extensive fractionization to achieve more accurate results because resolving power of analysis is insufficient to distinguish between sources that produce similar physical characteristics. *,†,‡,§*

b.   Edited version of the purpose-oriented abstract in 5a.

A 648-gram sample representative of roadway dust in a moderately large, nonindustrial urban community was subdivided by particle size, density, and ferromagnetic susceptibility, and subfractions were analyzed to determine major, minor, and trace elements. Results were subjected to multivariate statistical analysis to identify and quantify the sources in the sample. The roadway dust sample contained 76.0, 5.0, 0.3, 1.5, 7.7, 7.2, and 2.3 percent of soil, cement, salt, automobile-exhaust particles, iron, tire-wear particles, and unidentified substances, respectively. The combined use of statistical and quantitative analyses is recommended when characterizing urban roadway dust.

c. Findings-oriented version of the abstract in 5b.

The roadway dust in a 648-gram sample representative of that from a moderately large, nonindustrial urban community contained 76.0, 5.0, 0.3, 1.5, 7.7, 7.2, and 2.3 percent of soil, cement, salt, automobile-exhaust particles, iron, tire-wear particles, and unidentified substances, respectively. The sample had been subdivided by particle size, density, and ferromagnetic susceptibility, and subfractions had been analyzed to determine major, minor, and trace elements. Results were subjected to multivariate statistical analysis to identify and quantify the sources in the sample. The combined use of statistical and quantitative analyses is recommended when characterizing urban roadway dust.

Sample 6. Informative abstract composed from an article on psychophysiology.

a. Unedited purpose-oriented form. Key for suggested revisions to this unedited abstract: *, eliminate awkwardness; †, check sentence construction and achieve sentence variety; ‡, achieve conciseness.

The experimental work reported studied the phenomenon‡ of suggestibility *under four different forms of suggestion: indirect, auto-, hetero-, and conflicting.*‡ Healthy and ill students and patients, with and without autogenic training, were *tested with the Body Sway Test** to measure the effect of the suggestion. *The results were:* (a) *equally strong effects occurred under all four forms of suggestion;* (b) *autogenic training affected positive behavior on the Body Sway Test in both healthy and ill students;* (c) *the negative behavior in the Body Sway Test occurred when autogenic training was lacking;* (d) *under the conflicting suggestions, the behavior of the female patients was more positive than that of the male patients.*†‡

b. Edited version of the purpose-oriented abstract in 6a.

Suggestibility was measured under indirect, auto-, hetero-, and conflicting forms of suggestion by using the Body Sway Test. Healthy and ill students and patients, with and without autogenic training, were tested. Equally strong effects occurred under all four forms of suggestion. Autogenic training affected positive behavior on the test in both healthy and ill students. Negative behavior in this test occurred when autogenic training was lacking. The behavior of female patients was more positive than that of males under conflicting suggestions.

c. *Findings-oriented version of the abstract in 6b.*

Equally strong effects of suggestion occurred under indirect, auto-, hetero-, and conflicting forms when the Body Sway Test was given to healthy and ill students and patients, with and without autogenic training. Autogenic training affected positive behavior on the test in both healthy and ill students. Negative behavior in this test occurred when autogenic training was lacking. The behavior of female patients was more positive than that of males under conflicting suggestions.

PART V

PROFESSIONAL RELATIONSHIPS

INDICATIVE ABSTRACT:

Cooperative professional relationships between abstractors and other information-system professionals are discussed. Quality-control functions of users, sponsors, and managers of abstracting services are considered. Responsibilities of editors or reviewers of abstracts are described, including those of effectively communicating with, training, and evaluating abstractors, and improving the style and content of original English language and translation abstracts. The topics of abstracting as a profession and the professional status of access abstractors are examined.

Chapter 16

Communal-Professional Relationships in Information Science

Because you see, what has made science successful as a social leaven over the last three hundred years is its change from the practice of individuals, however great their ingenuity, to a communal enterprise.
—JACOB BRONOWSKI

Professional Relationships of Information Scientists

Much of the success of information scientists over the past 30 years can be attributed not only to their ingenuity as individuals but also to their communal or professional relationships. In addition to their relationships within the field of information science, almost all information scientists develop relationships within one or more of all the other scientific disciplines that they show allegiance to through education or practical experience.

As discussed by White and Griffith,[36] information scientists generally do their research in the broad subject areas of automated retrieval, document analysis, citation studies, bibliometrics, scientific and technical communications, and the evaluation of information systems. Like the late American artist Philip Guston, whom I quoted earlier, these scientists also experience individual, solitary "20-minute" creative spells in which they become intensively subjective while creating new technology and techniques to advance the state of the art in one or more of the research subject areas cited by White and Griffith. The frequency of these creative spells can be extremely variable, because most of these scientists must budget time for their research so as not to interfere with their primary occupations as information-system entrepreneurs and corporate executives, or as managers, consultants, or academicians. Holding a job in one of these occupations, of course, does not automatically qualify an individual as an information scientist. He or she must also contribute significant research findings in information science, as have Crawford, Fairthorne,

95

Garfield, King, Kochen, Lancaster, Lipetz, Luhn, Meadow, de Solla Price, and Saracevic, among others cited by White and Griffith.

In their more objective communal or professional relationships, information scientists interact with their colleagues indirectly through their published writings and directly through working, teaching, business, and social relationships, or through their associations as rank-and-file or active office-holding members of professional societies.

Professional Relationships of Information Specialists

Information specialists, including abstractors, indexers, bibliographers, translators, search analysts, lexicographers, editors, and other abstract-journal or information-processing, storage, and retrieval-system production workers, also maintain a community of professional relationships. Abstractors, when not experiencing their 20-minute spells of creative abstracting, maintain professional relationships with many of their fellow specialists. Abstractors for some information systems expand their professional relationships by doing additional specialty work as bibliographers, indexers, translators, editors, or contributors to the production control of abstract journals.

Many information specialists, like information scientists, share direct and indirect professional relationships with their colleagues through their own research and writing and through membership in many of the same professional societies.

Professional Interrelationships for Very Best Quality Abstracts

In my simple model for preparing good–better–best quality abstracts that I introduced in Part II of this book, I suggested that best-quality abstracts would invariably be written when the abstractor used good reading, thinking, writing, and editing skills while complying with the rules and conventions for abstracting. I added that the model could be extended to infer that what the abstractor had written could be transformed into very best quality abstracts when cooperative professional relationships were maintained. In the following final four chapters, I pursue this idea further by examining some of the direct and indirect interrelationships of abstractors with readers, information scientists, managers, editors, and other abstractors.

Chapter 17

Cooperative Management
of Abstracting and Abstractors?

Cooperative or Copyright Managing

The following copyright notice, printed in the front matter of all issues of *Chemical Abstracts*, protects the proprietary rights of the Chemical Abstracts Service to the abstracts and indexes on chemical and chemical engineering information that are produced by its editorial staff.

With this notice, management at Chemical Abstracts Service is using the copyright function as it was intended—to control access to their products and services. Most information-system managers do restrict their use of the copyright function to its intended purpose. These are potentially "cooperative" managers. Cooperative managers know that the policies and procedures for producing their information products are not static, figuratively copyrighted ones, subject only to rare adjustments based on a narrow set of "justifying circumstances," but are, in fact, dynamic ones requiring their constant attention, monitoring, and adjustment.

However, some information-system managers act as if they believe that their policies and procedures are rigidly fixed and are subject only to infrequent adjustments resulting from a narrow set of justifying circumstances. I consider these to be "copyright" managers. If the performance of abstractors and the quality of abstracts are continually to be improved, there must be an increase in the numbers of cooperative managers and a decrease in the numbers of "copyright" managers.

Product Awareness and Quality Control

In abstracting, product awareness is knowing what an acceptable abstract is, which actions are appropriate to minimize the publication and distribution of unacceptable abstracts, and when these actions should be taken. Product awareness and quality control should be concerns of everyone involved in the abstracting process—from users at the top, to sponsors and managers of abstracting services, editors or reviewers, and abstractors themselves at the source.

Users who identify inferior published abstracts should inform sponsors or managers of abstracting services so that they can take steps to improve the services. Sponsors who contract for abstracting services should familiarize themselves thoroughly with the fundamentals of abstracting and the value and limitations of abstracts. They should specify precisely the type, structure, style, and content of the abstracts that they prefer; monitor the quality of the abstracts that they receive; and promptly inform managers of abstracting services about significant shortcomings in their abstracts or lapses in procedures.

Managers of abstracting services should routinely make quality-control checks of abstracts and discuss with the editorial staff any problems that are identified. Editors or reviewers and abstractors should seek to identify and correct as many shortcomings as possible during the actual abstract-preparation process.

Selecting and Evaluating Abstractors

Undergraduate or graduate degree? Scientist or nonscientist? Specialist or generalist? Technologist or nontechnologist? Scholar or nonscholar? Linguist or nonlinguist? Indexer or nonindexer? Librarian or nonlibrarian? Who should be hired and trained to write access abstracts on scientific, technical, or scholarly subjects? Given the choice, most managers would, of course, prefer the better trained or more experienced candidates for abstracting jobs. But the higher the qualifications and the fewer the candidates, the greater the gap may be between salary needs and available funds, and the lower the potential will be for retention of the individual as an abstractor after he or she is trained. For these reasons, managers are often obliged to hire and train individuals with fewer qualifications than they might prefer.

Whether he or she seems highly or moderately qualified, as indicated by recommendations or résumé entries, once an access abstractor candidate is provisionally hired, it is imperative that his or her potential to write quality abstracts productively be determined. The manager therefore must evaluate new abstractors by using a set of performance criteria. In Chapter 15 of their monograph *Abstracting Scientific and Technical Literature: an Introductory Guide and Text for Scientists, Abstractors, and Management*,[21] Maizell et al. list twelve such criteria. These include factors such as promptness, accuracy, clarity, readability, completeness, and selectivity.

With the assistance of editors or reviewers, managers should be able to determine quickly how well a provisional abstractor can meet these and other performance criteria. After introductory training in abstracting fundamentals, the abstractor should be assigned three to five papers or mongraphs containing diverse subject matter for original abstracting. These materials should not contain author abstracts. If author abstracts have been published with the materials, they should be deleted on the copy used for abstracting by the trainees.

After they are abstracted by the new abstractor, the three to five abstracts should be carefully edited by an editor, reviewer, or senior abstractor. The superior should discuss the results with the new abstractor, emphasizing points on structure, style, unity, and conciseness. A second batch of twice as many materials for original abstracting should then be assigned, with possible inclusion of items from the first group that require extensive rewriting. After the resulting abstracts are edited, the manager should have a clear idea as to how long it will take the provisional abstractor to become proficient.

Chapter 18

Informal Notes to Editors of Abstracts

Besides self-editing, almost all abstracts receive further editing or reviewing before they are published, filed manually, or stored in computers. The editing or reviewing ranges from a minimal amount for camera-ready-copy abstracts, to a moderate amount for most conventional informative and indicative abstracts, to a very thorough pre- and post-publication review for some lengthy and highly detailed digests of long or complex primary documents.

Editors of abstracts may hold one of a variety of titles, including the general one of editor or reviewer on up to that of managing editor, with such intermediary titles as associate or assistant editor. Editors orally discuss abstracts and abstracting, or exchange notes or memoranda, with sponsors, managers, and voluntary, free-lance, or staff abstractors. The discussions and notes cover such topics as abstracting procedures, style, and content; deadlines; individual abstractor performance; and training. The notes on some of these and other topics that follow are addressed to all editors or reviewers of abstracts and trainers of abstractors, regardless of their titles.

Reading Rules for the Editor

The three interrogatory rules for self-editing of abstracts by use of critical reading also apply when additional editing is done by editors or reviewers. These three rules were discussed in Chapter 12.

Rule 1. Is the abstract properly structured and unified?
Rule 2. Is the content of the abstract complete, coherent, and concise?

Rule 3. Does the abstract conform to both general style rules and conventions for abstracts and to those special ones contained in the publisher's or information-system manager's instructions on the type and length of abstracts?

Two additional rules are proposed for editors and reviewers. Rules 4 and 5 concern actions to be taken when major or minor shortcomings are identified in the abstract.

Rule 4. Are there significant shortcomings in the style and content of the abstract that will require extensive revision and rewriting to make it acceptable for publication or storage for retrieval?

For abstracts that do contain major shortcomings, editors must decide whether routinely to edit the inferior abstract, and probably in the process spend more than the standard amount of time allotted for editing, or to return it to the abstractor for revision. Whenever it is feasible, the latter step is recommended because the responsibility for producing acceptable abstracts is properly placed with the abstractor. The quality of subsequent abstracts that he or she writes should improve, and the editor's productive time and ability to improve other abstracts are enhanced.

The fifth rule for editors and reviewers concerns the communication process between them and abstractors.

Rule 5. Should major shortcomings in style and content or recurring minor infractions of style rules and conventions for acceptable abstracts be brought to the attention of the abstractor?

Time permitting, editors of abstracts should attempt to point out all major shortcomings and recurring minor ones to abstractors by arranging for the shortcomings to be marked on edited copy and distributed to the abstractor, and through periodic reviews.

Elements of Communications Style

The development and maintenance of good-quality abstracting services requires routine, open, two-way communication between editors and abstractors. Paraphrasing Strunk and White's "omit needless words" advice for developing good writing style, I suggest that the basis for cooperative professional relationships between editors and abstractors during this communication process should be "omit needless conflicts." Whether splitting hairs over split infinitives, explaining the reasons for preferring either purpose- or results-oriented abstracts, or pointing out the major flaws in style and content that require the rewriting of an abstract, the editor must always be sensitive to the feelings of the abstractor and must avoid embarrassing him or her.

Each criticism worthy of being brought to the abstractor's attention should be accompanied by constructive advice for improvement or reference to written instructions containing such advice. Oral or written communications with abstractors should be timely and accurate, and should be carried out in a congenial, firm (but undogmatic) manner. Editors can gain significantly when there is a two-way flow of information on abstracting procedures. Besides verbal communication, the use of notes or memoranda is also beneficial. Standard forms from editors to abstractors similar to the one shown in Figure 13 can easily be converted for use by abstractors who wish to forward comments and questions on procedures and style to editors.

Style Points and Reminders for Abstractors (These style points or reminders result from the editing process and are forwarded to assist in maintaining a high degree of clarity, coherence, and conciseness in your abstracts.)
Abstracting (General):
Abstracts (Specific) Purpose: Methodology: Results-Conclusions-Recommendations: Other:
Abstractor _____ Date _____ Editor(s) _____

FIG. 13. *Sample form for style points and reminders.*

Continuing Education and Continuous Instruction

If abstracting is a form of continuing education with pay for abstractors, it is even more so for editors of abstracts. Editors who have had no prior training or experience as instructors must rapidly learn and apply many teaching techniques. For those who have had training or practical experience in teaching, the editing of abstracts serves as an excellent opportunity to apply and polish instructional skills.

To instruct effectively, editors must master not only the fundamentals of abstracting but also the three primary communication skills that comprise the subject—reading, writing, and editing. They must be knowledgeable enough to introduce the background materials on abstracting to trainees in a clear, comprehensive, and stimulating way. Editors must accurately evaluate the performance of abstractors during training and their progress after they become qualified. Moreover, editors must be capable of identifying the drawbacks of individuals who fail to respond to instruction within a reasonable period of time. This information should be recorded in evaluations to assist managers in deciding whether it will be counterproductive, both to the trainee and to the abstracting service, if he or she is retained.

Translation Abstracts

Abstracts written by those for whom English is a second language or abstracts written from poorly translated materials often serve as a difficult, but rewarding, challenge to the editor's critical reading skills. Communication with translators whose fluency in English is only fair is often an equally difficult challenge to the editor's skills as an instructor. Besides resolving standard editing and training problems, the editors in both situations also must remove the remaining language barriers that were not overcome during the translation process.

Editors should be particularly alert for the appearance of the following flaws in translation abstracts: nonstandard word choice (e.g., falling hair, poisoning, and radar impulses for alopecia, treatment, and radar pulses in abstracts of medical, toxicological, and communications research papers, respectively), ambiguity, lack of conciseness, awkward sentence structure, and faults in using articles and prepositions.

General Editing Style Points

A syntopical index to the literature on abstracting concepts was presented in Chapter 11. Editors of abstracts often also must refer to general guidebooks on style and usage. As a second reference aid for editors, Appendix 7 contains an index to select points of style in seven such guidebooks.

Chapter 19

Abstracting as a Profession

---

905 Help Wanted
ABSTRACTOR
International health publication. Familiarity with health sciences and college degree required. Foreign language preferred. Convenient location. Full time. Call 999-000 ext. 2460. EOE

Individuals find work as abstractors through referrals to openings in the field by persons involved in or familiar with access-information systems and publications, or in response to advertisements similar to the one shown above. In this chapter, subjective comments on the benefits and consequences of abstracting are presented, along with more objective information on how to enter the field and on professional training programs.

Assessment of Abstracting Impacts

The environmental-impact statements that I once abstracted for the journal *EIS: Key to Environmental Impact Statements* were frequently lengthy, and so were some of the early abstracts that were published. Part of the lengthiness of the abstracts resulted from attempts to summarize impartially the primary positive and negative environmental impacts of each project or program for which a statement had been published and circulated for public review. That training in impartial reporting has influenced the preparation of the following summary of a few of the pros and cons of choosing abstracting as an occupation.

Positive impacts of abstracting. Within access-information systems, abstracts are one of the most fundamental and significant writing forms. Abstracting is an excellent training experience for writing in other, more challenging forms, particularly within the field of information science. These forms include content analyses, state-of-the-art literature reviews, and technical proposals.

Abstractors influence the decision-making processes of indexers, researchers, and other writers, and contribute to their effectiveness as a function of the quality of the abstracts that they produce.

With each new document that is accepted for abstracting, the access abstractor is given an opportunity to master the information content within the document, to maintain high standards in quality, and to gain the satisfaction that comes from meeting deadlines.

Abstractors who are required to extract and record bibliographic information or to index the materials that they abstract can broaden the range and market value of their information-specialist skills.

Abstractors who are furnished with constructive evaluations from editors, managers, or readers of their abstracts either receive recognition for well-written abstracts or are given opportunities to improve their writing skills when shortcomings in their abstracts are brought to their attention.

Abstractors with translating skills can improve their language proficiency and technical-writing skills, both in familiar subject areas and in unfamiliar ones in which they may be requested to write abstracts because of a shortage of qualified translators. Translators also may derive satisfaction from the knowledge that they are contributing to worldwide dissemination of scientific findings and scholarly thought. The quality of their translations may be a deciding factor in determining whether additional resources will be invested in preparing full-text translations for the papers that they abstract.

Abstracting serves as a daily, on-the-job, continuing educational experience, primarily in analytical reading and secondarily in thinking, writing, and editing.

Negative impacts of abstracting. As was usually true with the projects and programs that were described in the environmental-impact statements that I abstracted, most of the positive impacts of work as an access abstractor can be counterbalanced with approximately reciprocal negative ones.

Writing concise, condensed versions of scientific and scholarly papers is hard work that requires mental energy, sustained concentration, and self-discipline. Full-time abstractors quickly become aware of this fact. Undergraduate and graduate students who sometimes attempt to fit an abstracting job into their academic schedules to help with tuition costs have found that, although the work is not as physically demanding as other part-time jobs that are available to students, abstracting frequently drains the supply of mental energy that they have budgeted for their studies. Professionals in other fields who write abstracts part-time as an avocation often find it difficult to meet deadlines, or regret that in meeting them they are left with little free time to pursue other leisure interests.

Writing abstracts is a low-profile profession. A few abstractors are identified by their names on the masthead or in parentheses at the end of their abstracts in certain abstract journals. More in keeping with their task of condensing information, still other abstractors are identified only by their initials when their abstracts are published. But the majority of abstractors receive recognition of their names or initials only from their editors, and not at all from the readers of their abstracts.

Abstractors are often expected to complete both sides of an information-data sheet. That is, besides writing the abstract for an article or book, they also may be asked to prepare an index and to extract and record the bibliographic information from the primary document, usually in accordance with lengthy, precise instructions. Compensation for such extra work is sometimes less than commensurate with the extra time and effort that are expended in accomplishing it.

When the abstract is indexed by someone other than the abstractor, he or she is open to criticism from the indexer for not writing the abstract in such a way that the indexer's work is made effortless. The quality of his or her abstracts also may be criticized by editors, information-retrieval analysts, supervisors, managers, and the users of the information service. Or, at the opposite extreme, and to the detriment of his or her development as a skilled abstractor, he or she may work for a service that emphasizes the need for the timely submission of completed abstracts while showing only superficial concern for their style and content.

When they combine the skills of abstractor and translator and apply the latter skills, abstractors may on rare occasions be expected to demonstrate the bilingual or multilingual fluency and technical expertise of simultaneous translators at the United Nations. For their efforts, however, they might be paid at a rate that is barely competitive with the pay received by the fictional émigré nobleman who is obliged to work as a doorman in his adopted country. When abstracting an occasional poorly translated paper for which the original text in the foreign language is not available, all abstractors may be obliged to use the highest editing skills combined with a touch of linguistic guess-work to prepare an acceptable abstract.

The access abstractor works almost exclusively with materials that have initially been published in primary journals or as books, special reports, or patents. Most of what is acquired by other information specialists for processing by access abstractors and indexers does possess enough lasting value to justify recording and storage in information-retrieval systems. But access services occasionally assign papers for abstracting and indexing in which the information value was so low in their primary existence that they should have ended that existence buried between the covers of the primary publication. However, the abstractor sometimes is expected to abstract all documents assigned without questioning their relative information value.

Finally, human abstractors are threatened with partial or full replacement by computer abstractors. Innumerable algorithms are being written and tested to instruct machines to read and write abstracts less mechanically, while using more real and less artificial intelligence.

These, then, are some of the benefits and consequences of writing abstracts. On balance, I consider the work to be challenging and educational with good potential for advancement to more demanding analytical and management assignments. But each person who is contemplating work as an abstractor should carefully assess both the consequences and the benefits before deciding to enter the field.

Turning Professional

Abstractors enter into the profession mainly from library- or information-science schools or programs, from other careers or academic majors, or from within the staffs of information services or systems.

Graduates of information-science or library-science programs would seem to be the most likely candidates to become professional abstractors. Most have completed survey or practical courses on the subject, and some have gained practical experience as free-lance abstractors while enrolled in graduate or undergraduate classes. A few professional librarians write occasional abstracts for public-, government-, or special-library collections; nevertheless, most librarians indicate that they prefer to pursue careers within other librarianship or information-science fields, for example, as catalogers, indexers, programmers, or information-retrieval analysts. Of those who write abstracts, many do so only on an interim basis primarily to supplement their incomes or to gain a working knowledge of abstracting to broaden their skills as information scientists or managers.

A more fruitful and diverse source of professional abstractors for secondary publications and information systems is that comprising university graduates from academic programs other than library or information science, or individuals crossing into the information-science field from careers other than librarianship. Abstractors in this group tend initially to be subject specialists rather than information specialists, but after gaining practical experience in abstracting, they qualify as both subject and information specialists. These abstractor candidates include recent graduates who have been unable to find challenging work in their chosen fields of study, retirees from other professions seeking second careers, and free-lancers who write abstracts to supplement their incomes from their primary occupations.

Among this second source of abstractors, those who stay in the profession long enough to become proficient in their work often continue to write abstracts for extended periods of time. Some eventually decide to make abstracting a full-time career.

A third and smaller group of abstractor candidates for secondary information services is provided by transfers from within the staffs of information systems and services. Data clerks, document-acquisition specialists, catalogers, indexers, and information-retrieval analysts are among the types of specialists who are potentially eligible for cross-training as abstractors.

Professional Training

The training of professional abstractors is conducted in four general locations: on campus in library- and information-science programs, on or off campus in continuing-education programs, in the home or other appropriate premises by self-instruction, and on site at information-processing centers.

Courses in abstracting are given at many universities and colleges that offer library- or information-science programs. The courses often include training in indexing. Some of the students in these programs simultaneously gain practical experience in abstracting by writing abstracts part-time, particularly when they attend classes at universities that are located in or near metropolitan areas in which firms that furnish abstracting services are congregated. Continuing-education short courses in abstracting, sponsored by universities, government agencies, or private enterprises, are given infrequently on and off campus.

Many free-lance abstractors teach themselves to abstract by using guidelines provided by primary publishers or access-information services. Free-lancers also may receive short-term training on the premises of access-information systems.

On-the-job training of full-time professional abstractors usually occurs within the facilities of abstracting and indexing services. This training normally comprises a short period of reading and familiarization with the objectives and instructions of a particular abstracting system, followed by the actual writing of abstracts in conformance with system instructions. Some on-the-job training programs include a short pretraining period involving proofreading or minor editing tasks to assist the abstractor candidate in gaining familiarity with the style and content of abstracts. Staff editors or senior abstractors instruct the trainees and monitor their progress until the new abstractors achieve the required level of proficiency.

Volunteer Abstractors

Once a good source of specialized abstracts, the ranks of volunteer abstractors are steadily decreasing in number and output. Rowlett reports[26] that *Chemical Abstracts* began publication in 1907 with 129 volunteer abstractors who presumably prepared almost all of the 11,847 abstracts published that year. The number of volunteer abstractors for this publication increased steadily to a peak of 3,292 in 1966, when they prepared 67% of the abstracts that the Chemical Abstracts Service (CAS) published that year.

In 1979, about 1,000 volunteer abstractors wrote only about 10% of the abstracts for *Chemical Abstracts*. Most of the remaining 90% of the total of more than 500,000 abstracts were produced in a single intellectual review of the documents, using on-line computer-assisted aids, at CAS offices in Columbus, Ohio, or at those of CAS associates in Nottingham, England.

Rowlett predicts a continuing decline in assignments for volunteer abstractors, a situation that may well be typical of all information-access systems that use or have used the services of these abstractors. He concludes, nevertheless, that the dedicated service of volunteer abstractors will probably always be required in some difficult subject areas and for documents in the less common languages.

Chapter 20

Apologetic or Confident Abstractors?

Five years ago I was almost apologetic. A lot has changed since then.

—FRANK BORMAN
President, Eastern Airlines

Five years ago in this case was 1976. At that time, Frank Borman, as an ex-astronaut who had been the command pilot of Apollo 8 on the first lunar orbital mission, had little to be apologetic about. But as president of Eastern Airlines he was feeling almost apologetic because "it was no secret that our service needed improving." By 1981, the Eastern Airlines advertising copy in which he is quoted proclaimed that a top-to-bottom effort within the company at improving services enabled Borman to replace his "almost apologetic" words with the confident boast: "I'll stack our service up against anyone's. . . . For the last two years, more people have chosen to fly Eastern than any other airline in the free world."

Five years ago, when my thoughts for writing this book were still in the embryo stage, besides the positive comments that I heard from some abstractors about the value of abstracting and the satisfaction to be found in writing abstracts, I heard many comments from others that would not promote the sale of abstracting services or convince many people to take up abstracting as an occupation. When they introduced themselves at professional or informal gatherings, some of the less positive abstractors confidently announced themselves as information specialists. But if pressed to name their specialty, some of them answered "almost apologetically" that they were abstractors. This situation has not improved much today as I complete this book.

Some of the apologetic abstractors whom I have met are well qualified with years of experience as abstractors—people who have nothing to be ashamed of regarding the quality of the abstracting services that they furnish. For a few of these, the apologetic note may stem from frustration over delays in moving on to more advanced writing or editing assignments. Some are still not convinced that abstracting is a fully professional use of their education and skills.

Other abstractors are apologetic because they realize that they are not writing abstracts effectively and do not have the will or desire to improve. These abstractors seem to be marking time,"waiting for COBOL" or some other computer program to take them out of their misery by writing their abstracts for them automatically.

Other than Borko and Bernier's 1975 monograph on abstracting concepts and methods,[8] abstractors who have turned to the literature on library and information science over the past five years for stimulating materials on the subject of abstracting have found little that is encouraging. In their 1979 guide to information science,[11] Davis and Rush, before they discuss computer-based abstracting systems, even speculate on whether humans are capable of writing good abstracts:

> Little is known about how or why human abstractors choose from the original article what they include in the abstracts that they produce. Neither is it clear to what extent human abstractors are consistent in abstract production. Perhaps more important, especially since there is no concrete answer to the question of what constitutes a good abstract, questions relating to human selection and consistency may be irrelevant. It is just possible that the abstracts produced by humans are not good. If so, then it would be undesirable to try to emulate the processes that humans use in abstracting, since such emulation would lead simply to a faster rate of production of consistently poor abstracts, which might be easy to produce, but difficult to sell.

I disagree, of course, with the speculation that the abstracts composed by humans inherently are not good. I am confident that tens of thousands of excellent abstracts are written among the hundreds of thousands that are published annually in hundreds of abstract journals. But I do agree with Davis and Rush's implication that there is much room for improvement. Perhaps a "top-to-bottom" effort at improving abstracting services is needed, similar to that performed at Eastern Airlines to upgrade their transportation services. If such an effort were carried out successfully, almost all abstractors might confidently, not apologetically, boast in two years' time: We'll stack our abstracting services up against anyone's and challenge programmers to write programs so that the computer can attempt to emulate us!

Self-Starting and Innovative Abstractors

What kind of abstractor performance is worth emulating? Two of my favorite appraisal terms for good performance are self-starting and innovative. Generally, I include these terms in my evaluation of those individuals who regularly begin their work promptly, do it effectively, and resolve most of the problems that they encounter. When they are stymied, they seek expert advice. If they are experienced abstractors, they give advice when it is requested from them and they are knowledgeable enough to do so; if not, they attempt to refer others to the best possible alternative sources.

More specifically, I would apply the terms self-starting and innovative to those abstractors who appear to be taking the following advice. When abstracting, observe all the rules of analytical reading, particularly those for self-editing by means of critical reading. (Many abstractors fail to do the latter.) Modify or edit author abstracts only when instructed to do so. Thus, when you are instructed to write an original abstract for a paper, monograph, or report that already contains an author abstract or summary, do so, and ignore the author abstract.

Those who do not follow this advice often produce "original" abstracts that resemble the authors' far too closely in style and content. Those who do follow this advice frequently are pleased to find that the specialized skills that they have developed as professional abstractors allow them to write abstracts that are more informative than the authors' and that have a structure and style which conforms closely to the specifications of the publisher or sponsor of the access-information system for which they are writing their abstracts.

Finally, I advise both author and access abstractors to endeavor always to construct well-construed abstracts (not merely extracts) that would please such advocates of abstracts as Arthur Koestler, who had this to say about abstracts and extracts in the introduction to his essay "The Art of Discovery and the Discoveries of Art."[19]

> It is technically difficult and sometimes impossible to convey a complex theory by quoting extracts from the original text. The alternative is to condense and summarise—to abstract rather than extract.

Glossary

The superscript numbers enclosed in parentheses are keyed to the References section at the end of the book and indicate that the definition is based on or was extracted from a definition in the cited work.

access abstracts   Collections of abstracts prepared for access publications, such as abstract (secondary) journals, and computer-based information-retrieval systems.

annotations   One or two sentence notations or explanations of the contents of documents or studies.

author abstracts   Abstracts that are published initially in primary publications; they are normally, but not exclusively, written by the authors of the published materials that they accompany. Author abstracts are frequently redistributed (intact or revised), copyright permitting, by access-information services.

cognition   1. Intellectual knowledge. 2. The act of knowing.[3]

computer-based abstracts   Abstracts that are partially or fully composed by using techniques for computer-assisted selecting, extracting, formatting, and printing of representative information.

critical abstracts   Abstracts that contain evaluative comments deliberately added by the abstractors on the significance of the material abstracted or the style of its presentation.

descriptive abstracts   See **indicative abstracts**

editing (abstracts)   Process by which abstractors, editors, and reviewers ensure that abstracts are unified and concise, that they contain an appropriate amount of accurate relevant information, and that they conform to conventional and special rules for writing abstracts.

extracts   Unedited representative portions of a document, usually in sentence form; used as basic materials for composing abstracts or as substitutes for them.

findings-oriented abstracts   Informative abstracts containing major results, conclusions, and/or recommendations in a topical first sentence, followed by sentences containing further results, conclusions, or recommendations and supporting details on methodology, purpose, or scope.[2,33]

highlight abstracts   Used by editors of journals to inform readers more

113

fully about the contents of articles in scientific, technical, and scholarly journals.[21]

indicative abstracts   Abstracts that contain descriptive information on purpose, scope, or methodology in documents on basic and applied research, reviews, and other printed or recorded materials, but no details of results, conclusions, or recommendations.

informative abstracts   Abstracts that contain key results, conclusions, or recommendations from documents resulting from basic or applied research and development. Information on methodology, purpose, or scope also may be included when important.

modular abstracts   Full content descriptions of documents prepared by subject specialists and resulting in an annotation; indicative, informative, and critical abstracts; and a set of modular index entries; designed to eliminate duplication and waste of intellectual effort and furnish a product of standardized format for partial or complete use by a variety of access services.[20]

professional relationships (cooperative)   Process through which abstractors, editors, reviewers, sponsors and managers of information systems, and users contribute to or monitor and advise on methods for developing and maintaining the highest standards of quality for the composition of abstracts, within the constraints of time and money.

purpose-oriented abstracts   Abstracts in which information on the primary objectives, scope, or methodology is presented before details of results, conclusions, or recommendations.

reader-oriented abstracts   Findings-oriented abstracts that, in access collections, place their bibliographical information at the ends of their texts.

reading (analytical)   Reading done to construct well-construed informative or indicative abstracts that reflect the use of clear thinking, concise writing of relevant information, and critical editing. Analytical reading for abstracting is done slowly in three sequential stages (retrieval, creative, and critical) by inexperienced abstractors and rapidly and less sequentially by proficient abstractors.

reviews   See **critical abstracts**

rules (abstracting)   Rules that control the style and content of abstracts and are based on guidelines in the *American National Standard for Writing Abstracts* and the specifications, instructions, or style manuals of primary publishers, sponsors, or managers of access abstracting services, as supplemented by general style points in manuals for lengthier forms of scientific, technical, and scholarly writing.

scope   Intent, import of a writing or discourse.[8]

statistical abstracts   Abstracts used for specialized subjects, such as thermophysical properties and economic data, where the emphasis is on the data. The abstract is a summary of the data in tabular form.[8]

summary   A brief restatement within a document (often at the end) of its salient findings and conclusions, intended to complete the orientation of a reader who has studied the full text. Because other vital portions of the document (for example, purpose or methodology) are not usually condensed into this type of summary, the term should *not* be used synonymously with "abstract."[2]

synoptics   A concise first publication in a directly usable form of key results selected from an available but previously unpublished paper. It differs from an abstract (which it contains) in that it is often a combination of text, tables, and figures, and may contain the equivalent of 2,000 words.[2]

terse conclusions   Conclusions expressed in concise elegance: "That which is used, develops; that which is not used, wastes away."[8]

thinking   1. A mental activity whereby a person uses concepts acquired in the process of learning and directs them toward some goal and/or object. 2. Any of the mental activities of which we are conscious, such as reflecting, inferring, remembering, introspecting, retrospecting, doubting, willing, feeling, understanding, apprehending, perceiving, meditating, imagining, pondering, etc.[3]

Appendix 1

Abstract of the *American National Standard for Writing Abstracts**

Abstract

An abstract is an abbreviated, accurate representation of the contents of a document, preferably prepared by its author(s) for publication with it. Such abstracts are also useful in access publications and machine-readable data bases. The following recommendations are made for the guidance of authors and editors, in order that the abstracts published in primary documents may be both helpful to the readers of these documents and reproducible with little or no change in access publications and services. If changes are required, however, many of the guidelines presented should prove useful.

Prepare an abstract for every formal item in journals and proceedings, and for each separately published report, pamphlet, thesis, monograph, and patent. Make the abstract as informative as the nature of the document will permit, so that readers may decide, quickly and accurately, whether they need to read the entire document. State the purpose, methods, results, and conclusions presented in the original document, either in that order or with initial emphasis on findings (results and conclusions).

Place the abstract as early as possible in the document, with a full bibliographic citation on the same page. Make each abstract self-contained, since it must be intelligible without reference to the document itself. Be concise without being obscure; retain the basic information and tone of the original document. Keep abstracts of most papers and portions of monographs to fewer than 250 words, abstracts of reports and theses to

---

fewer than 500 words (preferably on one page), and abstracts of short communications to fewer than 100 words.

Write most abstracts in a single paragraph, except those for long documents. Normally employ complete, connected sentences; active verbs; and the third person. Use nontextual material such as short tables and structural formulas only when no acceptable alternative exists. Employ standard nomenclature, or define unfamiliar terms, abbreviations, and symbols the first time they occur in the abstract.

When abstracts are employed in access publications and services, precede or follow each abstract with the complete bibliographic citation of the document described. Include pertinent information about the document itself (type, number of tables, illustrations, and citations) if this is necessary to complete the message of the abstract; here, complete sentences need not be used.

Appendix 2

Reading Rules for Abstracting

General Reading Rules for Abstracting

Rule 1. Read actively to identify information for the abstract and passively for understanding.

Rule 2. Read with standard rules and conventions and special instructions for writing abstracts in mind.

Rule 3. Read attentively through the full abstracting process of reading, thinking, writing, and self-editing.

Rule 4. Read with enthusiasm.

Retrieval Reading

Rule 1. Read quickly but attentively through the text of the material to be abstracted to identify passages containing information with potential for inclusion in the abstract.

Rule 2. While reading, mentally or in the margin of the copy note which parts of the material contain information on purpose, methods, findings, or conclusions and recommendations. (If you mark in the margins on manuscripts or published copies of materials being abstracted, write lightly in pencil so that the markings may be erased without damaging the copy.)

Creative Reading

Rule 1. (*Step A*) Reread all of the information on purpose, scope, and methods that you identified during the retrieval-reading process. While reading, mentally index the primary and secondary themes described in this material, using your own choice of arbitrary terms or phrases. (Beginning abstractors or those writing an abstract for a complex document might find it helpful to jot down their arbitrary index terms or phrases on note paper.) (*Step B*) Write the primary annotative part of the abstract (the first sentence).

Rule 2. From the remaining information on purpose, scope, and methods, extract appropriate materials and write the secondary annotative sentence or sentences.

If your instructions are to write an indicative abstract, you have now completed the creative-reading stage and are ready to begin the critical-reading stage for self-editing of the completed abstract. If you are writing an informative abstract, continue on to Rules 3 and 4.

Rule 3. (*Step A*) If you are writing an abstract of a document reporting on experimental research, tests, surveys, or case reports, reread the textual materials on the results or findings. While reading, condense this information mentally or write it on note paper to aid your judgment of its relevancy and significance. (*Step B*) Extract the most relevant results and write them in sentence form, concisely, in descending order of significance.

Rule 4. (*Step A*) Reread the conclusions and recommendations that were identified during the retrieval-reading process in a manner similar to that described in Rule 3. (*Step B*) Extract the most relevant conclusions and recommendations and write them in sentence form, tersely, in descending order of significance. (Application of this rule depends on whether it is required by publishers or managers of access-information systems.)

Critical Reading

Rules 1, 2, and 3 of critical reading are for abstractors; rules 4 and 5 are for editors and reviewers of abstracts.

Rule 1. Is the abstract properly structured and unified?

Rule 2. Is the content of the abstract complete, coherent, and concise?

Rule 3. Does the abstract conform to both general style rules and conventions for abstracts and to those special ones contained in the publisher's or information-system manager's instructions on the type and length of abstracts?

Rule 4. Are there significant shortcomings in the style and content of the abstract that will require extensive revision and rewriting to make it acceptable for publication or storage for retrieval?

Rule 5. Should major shortcomings in style and content or recurring minor infractions of style rules and conventions for acceptable abstracts be brought to the attention of the abstractor?

Appendix 3

Select Annotated
Bibliography on Abstracting

Annotations that are adapted from abstracts in *Information Science Abstracts* are appended with the *ISA* accession number for the modified abstract, e.g., *ISA*, 77-1642.

Quality

Ashworth, W. Abstracting as a fine art. *Information Scientist* 7(2):43–53, 1973

Abstracting is discussed as an activity calling for creativity and skill and having a susceptibility to formal analysis. Abstracts prepared with good literary style serve a useful purpose in improving communication, while providing a source of creative fascination to the abstractor.

Guidelines

Borko, H., and S. Chatman. Criteria for acceptable abstracts: a survey of abstractors' instructions. *American Documentation* 14(2):149–160, 1963

Instructions in 130 guides for abstractors were reviewed to develop criteria for judging the adequacy of human-produced abstracts initially and computer-produced abstracts subsequently, if necessary. An adequate abstract of a research article must cover purpose, method, results, conclusions, and specialized content.

McGirr, C. J. Guidelines for abstracting. *Technical Communication*, 2–5, Second Quarter, 1978

Advice on the preparation, review, content, and length of abstracts is presented. Abstracts should use definite statements, not generalities; short clear statements for each thought; and language familiar to the reader.

Weil, B. H., I. Zarember, and H. Owen. Technical-abstracting fundamentals. II. Writing principles and practices. *Journal of Chemical Documentation* 3(2):125–132, 1963

Guidelines are presented for writing findings- (reader-) oriented informative abstracts. Abstracts can serve their purpose best only if they are carefully written to transmit important information to readers quickly and accurately, which requires knowledge of audience needs, habits, and desires, and the ability to identify the key facts in the document, to organize these facts, and to write the abstracts clearly, concisely, and in conformity with the style rules of the medium involved.

Monographs

Borko, H., and C. L. Bernier. *Abstracting Concepts and Methods.* Academic Press, New York, 1975 (*ISA*, 77-1325)

The history, production, organization, and publication of abstracts are discussed. Instructions, standards, and criteria for abstracting are considered, along with information on management, automation, and personnel in terms of possible economies that can be derived from the introduction of new technology or management techniques.

Collison, R. L. *Abstracts and Abstracting Services.* A. B. C.-Clio, Inc., Santa Barbara, Calif., 1971 (*ISA*, 72-1627)

The mechanical production of abstracts, from abstractor to finished, edited, and indexed abstract is described.

Maizell, R. E., J. F. Smith, and T. E. R. Singer. *Abstracting Scientific and Technical Literature.* Wiley-Interscience, New York, 1971 (*ISA*, 72-2147)

A practical guide is presented on the writing, dissemination, and use of scientific and technical abstracts. The guide includes information on managing abstracting operations within a company or organization, the role of the abstractor in literature searching, and how an abstractor can use modern technology to facilitate the production and use of abstracts.

Automatic (Computer-Assisted) Abstracting

Borkowski, C. Structure, effectiveness and benefits of LEXtractor, an operational computer program for automatic extraction of case summaries and dispositions from court decisions. *Journal of the American Society for Information Science* 26(2):94–102, 1975 (*ISA*, 75-2226)

A computer program (extractor) for automatic extraction of case summaries and dispositions is described. The structure of LEXtractor, its cost and performance, and relevant issues in text editing are outlined.

Firschein, O., and M. A. Fischler. *Automatic Information Abstracting and Extracting. Part 2. Describing and Abstracting Pictorial Data.* Final Report LMSC-D350104-Pt-2., Palo Alto Research Laboratory, Lockheed Missiles and Space Co., Inc., Palo Alto, Calif., 1973 (*ISA*, 73-3490)

The manner in which people create and use descriptions of image data and how to combine different descriptions of the same picture to obtain an "encyclopedic entry" for the picture are discussed. (See also *Describing and Abstracting Pictorial Structures*, Report 1, under the heading "Nonstandard Abstracts" in this annotated bibliography.)

Mathis, B. A. *Techniques for the Evaluation and Improvement of Computer-Produced Abstracts.* The Computer and Information Science Research Center, The Ohio State University, Columbus, OSU-CISRC-TR-79-15, 1972 (*ISA*, 73-1644)

An automatic abstracting system (ADAM), implemented on an IBM 370, receives journal articles as input and produces abstracts as output, using an algorithm which considers all of the sentences in the input text and rejects those which are not suitable for inclusion in the abstract. The quality of the abstracts is evaluated by a two-step evaluation procedure.

Readability

King, R. A comparison of the readability of abstracts with their source documents. *Journal of the American Society for Information Science* 27(2):118–121, 1976 (*ISA*, 76-3396)

Readability levels of 30 items from child development abstracts and 30 passages from their corresponding journal articles were compared by a CAL SNOBOL computer program referenced to a CLOZE criterion. Results support the hypothesis that abstracts were more difficult to read than their source documents.

Kowitz, G. T., et al. From ERIC source documents to abstracts: a problem in readability. Presented at the Rocky Mountain Education Research Association, Tucson, Ariz., 29 November 1973 (*ISA*, 77-2174)

The Flesch RE formula was used to calculate readability scores for abstracts and their source documents that were selected randomly from four clearinghouses. Analysis of variance indicated that the abstracts were readable, but less so than the source documents.

Subject Slanting

Herner, S. Subject slanting in scientific abstracting publications. In *International Conference on Scientific Information, Washington, D.C., Proceedings, Vol. 1*, pp. 407–427. National Academy of Sciences-National Research Council, Washington, D.C., 1959

Abstracts of representative papers from 51 prominent scientific periodicals which were announced by nine major indexing and abstracting publications were analyzed to determine the feasibility of cooperative abstracting. Statistical analysis of the slanting of abstracts of papers having no author summaries or abstracts indicates that subject slanting of abstracts is rare.

Nonstandard Abstracts

Bernier, C. L. Terse-literature viewpoint of wordage problems—amount, languages, and access. *Journal of Chemical Documentation* 12(2):81–84, 1972 (*ISA*, 72-2144)

Terse conclusions and updatable handbooks or computer stores of data are discussed as ways of solving the problems of too much to read in the limited time available and of reading many foreign langauges. Terse conclusions may average 1% of the length of papers, act as surrogates, reduce backlog reading, speed use of literature, aid memory and research, be written rapidly, and be published inexpensively.

Bernier, C. L. Terse literatures. II. Ultraterse literatures. *Journal of Chemical Documentation and Computer Sciences* 15(3):189–192, 1975 (*ISA*, 75-3032)

The creation of ultraterse literatures (ULs), as demonstrated by reading a set of 30 terse conclusions (TCs), can be a part of generalization and the creation of new knowledge and research projects. Computers can probably be programmed to collect indexed TCs and to print out only those that exceed a figure of merit or a specified growth rate.

Broer, J. W. Abstracts in block diagram form. *IEEE Transactions on Engineering Writing and Speech* 14(3):64–67, 1971 (*ISA*, 72-1626)

A block diagram of interconnected word blocks with standardized titles and located in fixed positions of a two-dimensional information space contains condensed answers to what?, how?, and why? The arrangement aims at improving similarity between verbal structure and logical organization and at stimulating further work via multichannel input-output.

Firschein, O., and M. A. Fischler. *Describing and abstracting pictorial structures.* Report 1, MSC-6-80-70-37A, Palo Alto Research Laboratory, Lockheed Missiles and Space Co., Inc., Palo Alto, Calif., 1970 (*ISA*, 72-2145)

Three classes of formal descriptions of photographic materials are considered: grammar-based, which uses a set of rules to describe the arrangements and relationships among the picture primitives; descriptor-based, which captures the content of the picture by using terms or phrases; and procedure-based, in which a system (possibly grammar-based) capable of generating a large number of descriptions is coupled to a high-level control mechanism which selects procedures and order of procedures so as to produce only a single desired description.

Lancaster, F. W., and S. Herner. Modular content analysis. *Proceedings of the American Documentation Institute* 1:403–405, 1964

Full content descriptions of documents that result in an annotation; indicative, informative, and critical abstracts; and a set of modular index entries are proposed. The descriptions would eliminate duplication and waste of intellectual effort and furnish a product of standardized format.

Lunin, L. F. The development of a machine-searchable index-abstract and its application to biomedical literature. In Barbara Flood (ed.), *Three Drexel Information Science Research Studies*, pp. 47–134. Drexel Press, Philadelphia, 1967 (*ISA*, 68-272)

A mini-abstract is described which conveys to the reader key facts reported in biomedical documents, uses no coding, can be searched by the computer, and produces by-products, such as the pilot edition of the trace metals literature index-handbook. The mini-abstract is formed from words selected from a controlled vocabulary and placed in an order that resembles an English language sentence.

Appendix 4

Select Annotated Bibliography on Thinking and Cognition

Annotations that are adapted from those in *An Annotated Bibliography on Technical Writing, Editing, Graphics, and Publishing: 1950–1965*[25] are appended with appropriate accession numbers from that publication, e.g., B-1623.

Thinking (Monographs)

Peterson, M. S. *Scientific Thinking and Scientific Writing*. Reinhold, New York, 1961 (B-1543)

The traditional inductive reasoning process, the logic of several special methods, the role of hypothesis, and the general pattern of a complete scientific investigation in relation to the development of a professional background are discussed. The key to good writing is proper organization: grammar, spelling, and punctuation are of secondary importance.

Guyer, B., and D. A. Bird. *Patterns of Thinking and Writing*. Wadsworth, San Francisco, 1959 (B-1898)

Three related concepts are considered: language gives shape to thought which emerges in and through language, thought and language must pattern together to create meaning, and the mechanism for the creation of meaning is manipulation of those patterns constituting the symbolic conventions of the language.

Berthoff, A. E. *Forming, Thinking, Writing: the Composing Imagination*. Hayden Book Co., New York, 1978

Logical and rhetorical principles are presented in conjunction with exercises in composing to show how the choices we make when we write can be made more intelligently and with a greater sense of control if we have a method. The making of meaning is the work of the active mind, of what used to be called the imagination—that power to create, to discover, to respond to forms of all kinds.

Beardsley, M. C. *Thinking Straight: Principles of Reasoning for Readers and Writers.* Prentice-Hall, Inc., Englewood Cliffs, N.J., 1975

Critical or straight thinking for problem solving that conforms to the general principles of logic is discussed. Critical thinking is impossible without skill in handling language: analyzing and distinguishing meanings, grasping the significance of grammatical constructions, comprehending the basic structure of thought in a paragraph or series of paragraphs.

Flesch, R. *The Art of Clear Thinking.* Harper, New York, 1951 (B-1629)

Drawing from psychology, linguistics, anthropology, neurology, sociology, and other fields of science, findings on thinking and problem solving are discussed.

Weinland, J. D. *How to Think Straight.* Littlefield, Adams and Co., Totowa, N.J., 1972

Creative thinking is analyzed and common mistakes and fallacies in problem solving are described. Precepts, concepts, and generalizations are intelligible tools to explain the relationship of fact to theory.

Waller, T. G. *Think First, Read Later! Piagetian Prerequisites for Reading.* International Reading Association, Newark, Del., 1977

The hypothesis is examined that thinking, as basic psychological process or processes, is fundamental to and necessary for reading and that reading cannot be understood until it is considered in a "thinking" context and its relationship to these more basic processes is understood.

Thinking (Articles)

Pacifico, C. Thinking on thinking. *ChemTech*, February 1974, pp. 33–39; March 1974, pp. 147–152; June 1974, pp. 340–343; July 1974, pp. 406–411

The thinking process is discussed in terms of thoughts, facts, objects, relationships, and their interrelationships. To minimize erroneous thinking we must first characterize correct thinking.

Woodford, F. P. Sounder thinking through clearer writing. *Science* 156(3776):743–745, 1967

A graduate course on scientific writing can, if appropriately designed, strengthen scientific thinking through amelioration of inward confusion of thought. Experience in conducting such a course is disussed.

Glucksberg, S. The problem of human thought. *American Scientist* 53:299–301, 1965

Three books on thinking are reviewed: *Thinking: from Association to Gestalt* by J. M. Mandler and G. Mandler (a brief and delightful introduction to the history of the problem of thinking); *The Act of Creation* by A. Koestler (brilliant analogy rampant on a field of ingenious speculation); and *Structure and Direction in Thinking* by D. E. Berlyne (a neoassociationistic approach to directed thinking).

Lang, C. H. Clear thinking and its relationship to clear writing. Institute in Technical and Industrial Communications, Fifth Annual Proceedings, pp. 11–17, 1962 (A-0395)

Effective communication through clear thinking is discussed. Unclear thinking in writing is revealed through confusion of fact with nonfact, failure to assign precise meaning to words, and the drawing of conclusions which are unwarranted by the facts.

Skinner, S. B. Cognitive development: a prerequisite for critical thinking. *Clearing House* 49:292–299, 1976

The educational objective of teaching students to think critically is considered. Classroom and testing activities of value in fulfilling this objective are described.

Nalimov, V. V. Language and thinking: continuity vs. discontinuity. In *In the Labyrinths of Language: a Mathematician's Journey*, pp. 175–199. ISI Press, Philadelphia, 1981

The relevance of language and consciousness in the continuity of thinking is discussed, with emphasis placed on the semantics of rhythm as a direct access to continuous streams of consciousness. Analyses of comprehension on logical and extralogical levels and of the dialectics of continuous and discrete streams and states of consciousness indicate that the internal deep state of consciousness is unique in its essential continuity, which cannot be reduced to the discreteness of language; and statements made in a discrete language are constantly interpreted on a continuous level.

Cognition (Monograph)

Reitman, W. R. *Cognition and Thought: an Information-Processing Approach.* John Wiley & Sons, Inc., New York, 1965

The psychological implications of information-processing concepts and computer simulation are examined. Information-processing theories examine cognitive representations and processes and emphasize the functional properties of thought and the things it achieves.

Cognition (Articles)

Walker, D. E. The organization and use of information: contributions of information science, computational linguistics and artificial intelligence. *Journal of the American Society for Information Science* 32(5):347–363, 1981

Learning, problem solving, and decision making as they relate to knowledge synthesis and interpretation are discussed with emphasis on information storage and retrieval. New developments in computer-based procedures for working with concepts of information, knowledge, and language can improve our understanding of how people organize and use information.

Simon, H. A. Information-processing models of cognition. *Journal of the American Society for Information Science* 32(5):364–377, 1981

Progress in modeling human cognitive processes using computer programming languages as a formalism for modeling and computer simulation of the behavior of the systems modeled is reviewed. Modeling of cognitive processes tends to go on nearly independently at two levels: the level of complex tasks and the level of elementary processes.

Monsell, S. Representations, processes, memory mechanisms: the basic components of cognition. *Journal of the American Society for Information Science* 32(5):379–390, 1981

Investigations of the perception of objects and words, the distinction between short- and long-term memory mechanisms, the retrieval of remembered episodes and facts, and attention, performance, and consciousness are described. The understanding of human cognition is of increasingly critical importance in view of the need to design external information-processing and transmitting systems so that they will mesh with the cognitive capacities of their users.

Owen, P. A hierarchical information analysis of cognition and creativity. In *Progress in Cybernetics and Systems Research Volume IV. Cybernetics of Cognition and Learning Structure and Dynamics of Socioeconomic Systems, Health Care Systems, Engineering Systems Methodology*, p. 85–96. Halsted Press, New York, 1978 (*ISA*, 78-4826)

A cybernetic approach to cognition and creativity is described. Creativity is not lost in the process of expanding cognition: cognition waits for creativity; it does not destroy it.

Appendix 5

Creative Reading for Sample Abstract A (Continued from Chapter 9)

Purpose, Scope, and Methods

[Paragraph 3] If the same ratio of *cis*-epoxide to aldehyde obtained from the *cis*-3-hexene is maintained in the *trans*-3-hexene products, the residual aldehyde presumed to arise from the *trans* intermediate may be calculated. . . . This factor was used to calculate the ketone residual from the *cis* complex, starting with the *cis*-4-octene. [INDEX TERMS: *cis-trans* isomerism, aldehydes, olefins, residuals, calculations]

[Paragraph 5] A direct comparison between methyl and ethyl migrations is desirable if their relative rates are to be established; this can be done through the use of 3,4-dimethyl-3-hexene (DMH). . . . Both *cis*- and *trans*-3,4-dimethyl-3-hexene were used. The two ketone products, 4,4-dimethyl-3-hexanone and 3-ethyl-3-methyl-2-pentanone, will be referred to as I and II. The use of 3-ethyl-2-methyl-2-pentene (MEP) furnishes further data for assessing the validity of the concept of relative rates of migration of groups in establishing the product ratios. [INDEX TERMS: group migration, hydrogen atoms, methyl groups, ethyl groups, *cis–trans* isomerism, product ratios]

[Paragraph 6] Reactions were effected at 90°K in the apparatus routinely used for this purpose. The olefins were diluted 10 to 1 with propane. The exposure time to oxygen atoms was 5 min, and about 1% of the olefin was reacted. The products were determined, after warmup, on a column (0.25 in. × 12 ft glpc) of Carbowax-6000, at 135° and a helium flow of 100 cc/min. The *cis* and *trans* isomers of 3,4-epoxy-3,4-dimethylhexane were not separable. Ketones I and II were easily separable. Retention times were determined with authentic samples of the two ketones. [INDEX TERMS: reactions, low temperature, olefins, oxygen addition, *cis–trans* isomers, retention time]

[Table I] Fractional Product Yield for the O(^{3}P) Addition to Internal, Straight-Chain Olefins at 90°K . . . Products . . . 2-Butene, 2-Pentene, 3-Hexene, 4-Octene . . . *trans*-Epoxide, *cis*-Epoxide, Aldehyde, Ketone, *trans*-Epoxide/ketone, *cis*-Epoxide/aldehyde, *cis*-Epoxide/*trans*-epoxide, Total epoxide/total carbonyl . . . The olefins were diluted 10:1 in propane prior to condensation on a 100-cm^2 Pyrex surface. Sum of 2-propylpentanal and *cis*-4,5-epoxyoctane, not separated on the gas-liquid chromatography. [INDEX TERMS: fractional product yields, oxygen addition, straight-chain olefins, low temperature, epoxides, aldehydes, ketones, *cis–trans* isomerism, dilution, condensation, gas-liquid paper chromatography]

Results

[Paragraph 2] Comparison of the *trans*-epoxide to ketone ratios from the *cis*- *vs.* the *trans*-olefin with increasing size of the olefin indicates that these ratios diverge. However, the larger olefins show greater stereospecificity in their reactions. Thus, *cis*-3-hexene gives about 2.5 times as much *cis*-3,4-epoxyhexane as the *trans*-epoxide. [INDEX TERMS: *trans*-epoxide to ketone ratios diverged; greater stereospecificity for larger olefins]

[Paragraph 6] For all three olefins, only three gas-liquid paper chromatography peaks were obtained for the products. These corresponded to the epoxides and the ketones I and II. [INDEX TERMS: olefin gas-liquid paper chromatography peaks corresponded to epoxides and ketones]

Conclusions

[Paragraph 2] Even a relatively small quantity of 3-hexanone from the *cis* intermediate could easily account for the difference in the *trans*-epoxide/ketone ratio between the reactions of *cis*- and *trans*-3-hexene. It is noted that the recently proposed "epoxide-like" transition complex implies that, although only one form of the complex is possible from the *trans*-, two forms are possible from the *cis*-olefin. . . Of these, form b could readily lead to the ketone, because of easy migration of H, but form a would be expected to preponderate from the energetic viewpoint. [INDEX TERMS: effect of 3-hexanone on *trans*-epoxide/ketone ratio]

[Paragraph 3] An indication of the importance of these forms, within the framework of the transition states specified and the assumption that form a gives only the aldehyde in its rearrangement to the carbonyl end product, whereas form b gives mostly ketones, is obtained from the data of Table I. . . . Clearly, aldehyde formation from the *trans* intermediate is negligible. All of the straight-chain olefins of Table I conform to this generalization. . . . The correct value, 2.3, is obtained from *trans*-4-octene, because a contribution from the *cis* complex possible is virtually absent. . . . Although the *cis*-epoxide and aldehyde were not separated, the ratio of the two may be assumed to be the same as the corresponding one from *cis*-3-hexene. . . . It may be concluded that of the two forms of the transition complex derived from the *cis*-olefin, form a is the principal one and b is unimportant. [INDEX TERMS: negligible aldehyde formation from *trans* intermediate for all straight-chain olefins]

[Paragraph 4] Two generalizations are apparent from Table I. The first is that retention of configuration of products becomes more pronounced with increasing chain length of the olefin. The second is that reaction of oxygen atoms in the low-temperature region tends to be more stereospecific with *trans*- than with *cis*-olefins. A stereotransformation of the transition intermediate requires a rotation of 180°, about the modified olefinic bond, of one of the carbon atoms of the double bond with its attached groups. Obviously, this process occurs with the *cis*-olefins. The extent to which stereotransformation will occur depends on the rates of ring closure and the rates of rearrangements leading to final products, compared to the rate of *cis–trans* interchange in the complex. It seems reasonable to postulate that the rate of ring closure is independent of the size of the olefin. The ratio of total epoxide to total carbonyl products shows little change with size, and, hence, the rate of rearrangement to carbonyls is also size independent. The frequency of rotation of the portion of the complex . . . is then directly proportional to the extent of stereotransformation observed in the products. A measure of these transformations is the ratio of *cis*- to *trans*-epoxide, tabulated in Table I. . . . Qualitatively, it would be expected that because of the higher moment of inertia associated with the larger olefin, the stereospecificity should increase with size; this is indeed the case. It is interesting that *cis*-2-pentene shows more stereospecificity than *cis*-2-butene. Despite the fact that both compounds have a methyl group adjacent to the olefinic site, a larger rotational barrier is inferred to be associated with the 2-pentene. A quantitative consideration of the relationship of size and stereo effects would require that potential barriers for rotation be taken into account also, but the qualitative conclusions remain unaffected. [INDEX TERMS: retention of configuration of products with increasing olefin chain length; oxygen atom reactions more specific with *trans* olefins; stereotransformation of transition intermediate; stereotransformation and ring closure; rearrangement to carbonyls; stereospecificity increases with size]

[Paragraph 5] (The same two ketones are produced from MEP as from *cis*- and *trans*-DMH.) The important difference is that, whereas I results from the reactions of DMH with a rearrangement wherein a methyl group migrates, it is the migration of the ethyl group that gives I from MEP. . . . Therefore, if independent rates of migration are to be associated with these alkyl groups, the ketone ratio (I/II) produced from *cis*- or trans-DMH should be equal to (II/I) formed from MEP. It is emphasized that this follows if the presumed migration rates determine the position at which the O becomes localized. On the other hand, strong forces favoring addition to one of the olefinic carbons could control the alkyl group migrations. [INDEX TERMS: addition to olefinic carbons and migration of alkyl groups]

[Paragraph 7] The notable feature of these results is that, of the two ketones, I and II, I is the major product: (I/II) = 2.5:1. Furthermore, this ratio is virtually independent of the starting olefin. Thus, the concept of independent rates of migration of groups in the rearrangement occurring in the O atom addition to olefins *must be abandoned.* The other alternative would require that the directive effect of the alkyl groups in MEP is such that the O adds to the carbon with the two ethyl groups 2.5 times more rapidly than to the carbon with the two methyl groups. It would appear that, insofar as the ratio of ketones is concerned, it is their relative stabilities that control the rearrangement processes. Transformation to final products is a migration of an alkyl group concerted with the localization of the oxygen atom on one of the carbon atoms. Localization of the oxygen atom in the transition complex *preceding* alkyl group rearrangement is not in accord with the experimental results. If, in fact, localization did occur, the migration would be determined, in part (completely, if, as in MEP, the groups bonded to each of the olefinic carbon atoms occurred in pairs), by the directive factors, such as electron densities that are postulated as controlling the site of addition. . . . For MEP, addition of the O atom to that carbon atom of the double bond to which the two methyl groups are attached would be expected to be favored. Ketone II would, perforce, be formed in greater amounts than I; the data show unequivocally that this is incorrect. [INDEX TERMS: no independent group migration rates in rearrangements from O addition to olefins; ketone stability and control of rearrangement processes; final products via alkyl group migration and localization of oxygen atom on carbon atom]

[Paragraph 8] The concerted rearrangement, in which oxygen localization and group migration occur, requires both electronic and spatial reorganization. The addition of ground-state, triplet oxygen to singlet-state olefin to give singlet-state products requires a relaxation process, as represented by a crossing of states on a potential surface. The recently introduced representation of the initial transition intermediate as a loose epoxide structure seems especially appropriate. Migration of groups probably involves a transient bridging of the double bond carbon pair. The path by which the intermediate relaxes to final products could even involve steric effects. The formation of the grouping . . . in II is sterically less favorable than . . . in I, and it may be speculated that the preponderance of I over II in the reactions of the *cis*- and *trans*-DMH and MEP can be ascribed to such steric effects. [INDEX TERMS: electronic and spatial reorganization; transient bridging; steric effects]

[Paragraph 9] Table II shows an interesting variation among the three olefins as regards the epoxide/ketone ratio. The interpretation of these results, and, particularly, why MEP exhibits such a high epoxide/ketone ratio, is not yet at hand. [INDEX TERM: epoxide/ketone ratios]

Appendix 6

Creative Reading for Sample Abstract B (Continued from Chapter 10)

Purpose, Scope, and Methods

[Paragraph 2] Forrester, a professor at M.I.T.'s Sloan School of Management, relies on a computer model he developed to simulate the growth, decline, and stagnation of a hypothetical city (or "urban area") from birth to old age (250 years). . . . In his first chapter Forrester warns the reader that caution should be exercised in applying the model to actual situations. Subsequently, however, he expresses few reservations about the model's validity and freely uses it as a basis for prescribing public policy. [INDEX TERMS: computer model; simulation; urban growth/decline; public policy]

[Paragraph 3] The hypothetical city in *Urban Dynamics* is, in Forrester's words, "a system of interacting industries, housing, and people." At the start of the simulations there is only new industry in the city, but as time passes enterprises mature and then decline. The speed of this aging process depends on conditions in the city. As businesses pass through these successive stages, they employ fewer workers and a smaller proportion of skilled workers. [INDEX TERMS: industries; housing; workers]

[Paragraph 4] There are similarly three kinds of people in the city: "managerial-professional," "labor" (skilled or high-income workers), and "underemployed" (including unemployed and unskilled workers). And there are three kinds of housing, corresponding to the three kinds of people: premium housing, worker housing, and underemployed housing. [INDEX TERMS: management; employment; industries; housing; workers]

[Paragraph 5] The criteria used in evaluating the performance of the hypothetical city and the efficacy of alternative public policies are never explicitly set forth. However, minimization of taxes per capita would be a fair rendering of the underlying criteria. Forrester seems to think that the objective of the city is to produce the lowest possible tax rate. [INDEX TERMS: performance evaluation; taxes; supply side fiscal policy]

[Paragraph 6] The fiscal relationships in Forrester's urban system are intricate, but can be reduced to three fairly simple propositions: (1) Low-income households cost the city more in taxes than they pay, whereas the city makes a profit on high-income households. (2) Growing business enterprises are an unqualified good because they pay taxes and, by assumption, cost the city nothing in services. (3) Increases in local taxes and increases in local government expenditures produce "adverse" changes in the city's population and employment structure. It follows from these propositions that "urban-management policies" should be designed to encourage new enterprises and managerial-professional people to locate in the city and discourage low-skilled people from living there. [INDEX TERMS: financing, income, taxes, management planning]

[Paragraph 7] The influence of tax rates on employment and population structure in Forrester's city is powerful and pervasive. "Managerial-professional" and "labor" families are assumed to be repelled by high tax rates, whereas the "underemployed" are indifferent to them. High tax rates, moreover, discourage the formation of new enterprises and accelerate the aging of existing ones. There are still other adverse effects: high taxes retard construction of both premium and worker housing, which in turn discourages the kinds of people who live in these kinds of housing from moving to the city or remaining there. [INDEX TERMS: taxes, effects; employment; population; housing]

[Paragraph 8] Increases in public expenditures, the other half of the local fiscal equation, also have disastrous effects on the system. It is assumed that increases in expenditures per capita make the city no more attractive to high-income people and new enterprises, but make it substantially more attractive to low-income people. There are some small offsets in the positive effects of higher expenditures per capita on upward mobility from the underemployed class into the labor class; but these are overwhelmed by the direct and indirect effects on the size of the underemployed population. [INDEX TERMS: public financing, mobility, employment]

[Paragraph 9] These examples are only a few of the "adverse" consequences of higher taxes and increased public expenditures in Forrester's model. Since the model is so constructed that a development in one sector affects other sectors, these adverse effects cumulate throughout the system. [INDEX TERMS: taxes, public financing]

[Paragraph 10] Forrester uses his simulation model to evaluate several "urban-management programs" that have been tried or proposed, and he concludes that they "may actually worsen the conditions they are intended to improve." For example, he finds that "financial support from the outside"—presumably including revenue sharing by the federal government—"may do nothing to improve fundamental conditions within the city and may even worsen conditions in the long run." But this conclusion is not at all surprising in view of what he does with the outside funds. Rather than using them to reduce or hold down city taxes, as proponents of such intergovernment transfers envision, Forrester uses them to increase city expenditures. Given the framework of his model, the net effects are inevitably adverse. [INDEX TERMS: computer model; evaluation; urban models; financing, external; taxes; municipal expenditures]

[Paragraph 11] But Forrester considers only the favorable effects of the demolition program. Given his model, these are considerable. The induced shortage of low-income housing makes the city less attractive to low-income people; fewer come and more leave. (Where they go is a question the model is not designed to consider). As before, a decline in the ratio of "underemployed" to total population makes the city more attractive to high-income people, encourages formation of new enterprises and construction of premium and worker housing, and impedes deterioration of dwelling units and businesses. In addition, the land cleared by increased demolition of low-income housing provides space for new enterprises and for premium and worker housing. [INDEX TERMS: taxes; costs; housing; mobility; employment; urban decline]

Conclusions/Recommendations

[Paragraph 2] Before adequate models become available, many inadequate ones will be put forward. Forrester's model is a conspicuous example. [INDEX TERMS: inadequate model]

[Paragraph 10] If instead Forrester had used the outside support to reduce city taxes, the net effects would have been favorable to the hypothetical city. Virtually all of Forrester's evaluations of "conventional" policies are similarly flawed; none is a faithful rendering of policies it supposedly represents. [INDEX TERMS: inferior evaluation of municipal fiscal policies]

[Paragraph 11] Considering the heavy emphasis Forrester puts on tax rates, it is striking that he fails to consider the costs of his principal recommendation: each year demolish 5 percent of the low-income housing. The costs of acquiring and demolishing the properties would increase city taxes, and, within the framework of the model, any increase in city taxes has adverse effects. But Forrester considers only the favorable effects of the demolition program. [INDEX TERMS: failure to include cost of annually demolishing a percentage of low-income housing]

[Paragraph 12] Given the critical role of land availability in the model, it would appear that these adverse effects could be staved off if the city could simply extend its boundaries so as to absorb additional vacant land; but Forrester does not deal with this possibility. [INDEX TERMS: failure to predict use of vacant land beyond city limits]

[Paragraph 13] Simplification is essential in computer simulation models, and neither Forrester's nor any other model can be criticized merely because it omits detail. But Forrester omits some basic behavioral relationships. The model's most serious weakness is that the suburbs never explicitly appear in it. For some simulation purposes, it might be permissible to disregard temporarily the interrelations between, say, the city and the rest of the nation beyond the metropolitan area. But what happens in a city strongly influences its suburbs, and vice versa. If the central city reduced its low-income population by 100,000, the low-income population of the suburbs would have to increase by roughly the same amount. Although Forrester's model reflects no awareness of this aspect of metropolitan interdependence, suburban governments are all too aware of it. Indeed, much of the urban problem today is a result of suburban governments' successfully pursuing precisely the kind of begger-thy-neighbor policies Forrester advocates for the central city. [INDEX TERMS: no explicit mention of reciprocal urban and suburban effects]

[Paragraph 14] Upon scrutiny, *Urban Dynamics* amounts to an intricate attempt to justify the responses of big-city mayors to a harsh fiscal environment. Existing intergovernmental arrangements saddled them with awesome responsibilities for the nation's social problems, but failed to provide them with commensurate financial resources. Much of the mayors' enthusiasm for now much-criticized urban-renewal programs is traceable to their desperate need for cash. In *Urban Dynamics*, pragmatic responses to an unbalanced allocation of responsibilities and tax resources are elevated to the status of rational and efficient policies for dealing with the complex web of problems popularly referred to as the "urban crisis." [INDEX TERMS: misinterpretation of significance of pragmatic financing of urban renewal programs]

[Paragraph 15] The solution is not, as Forrester indicates, the pursuance of narrow self-interest by each local government. Instead we need to develop a more appropriate division of responsibilities and functions among governments, and thereby remove the fiscal incentives for local governments to follow policies that, while perhaps efficient from the viewpoint of narrow self-interest, are inefficient from the viewpoint of society as a whole. [INDEX TERMS: recommend redistribution of municipal responsibilities and functions]

Appendix 7

Index to Points of Editing Style

In the seven citations presented the number preceding the colon represents one of the following five references; the numbers following the colon represent pages in the reference cited.

1. Bernstein, T. M. *The Careful Writer: a Modern Guide to English Usage.* Atheneum, New York, 1973
2. CBE Style Manual Committee. *Council of Biology Editors Style Manual: a Guide for Authors, Editors, and Publishers in the Biological Sciences,* 4th ed. Council of Biology Editors, Inc. (distributed by American Institute of Biological Sciences, Arlington, Va.), 1978
3. Day, R. A. *How to Write and Publish a Scientific Paper.* ISI Press, Philadelphia, 1979
4. Follett, Wilson. *Modern American Usage,* edited and completed by Jacques Barzun in collaboration with Carlos Baker et al. Warner, New York, 1966
5. Kierzek, J. M., and W. Gibson. *The Macmillan Handbook of English,* revised by R. F. Willson, Jr., 6th ed. Macmillan, New York, 1977
6. Perrin, P. B., and G. H. Smith. *The Perrin-Smith Handbook of Current English,* 2nd ed. Bantam, New York, 1966
7. Strunk, W., Jr. *The Elements of Style,* with revisions, an introduction, and a chapter on writing by E. B. White, 3rd ed. Macmillan, New York, 1979

Terms

When/If   *see* If/When
Which/That   *see* That/Which
While   1:476–477; 4:442–443; 5:490; 6:55, 58; 7:63–64
Who/Whom/Whoever/Whomever   1:477–479; 4:443–446; 5:491

References

1. Adler, M. J., and C. Van Doren. *How to Read a Book: the Classic Guide to Intelligent Reading.* Simon and Schuster, Inc., New York, 1972
2. American National Standards Institute, Inc. *American National Standard for Writing Abstracts.* ANSI Z39.14-1979. American National Standards Institute, Inc., New York, 1979
3. Angeles, P. A. *Dictionary of Philosophy.* Harper & Row, New York, 1981
4. Ashworth, W. Abstracting as a fine art. *Information Scientist* 7(2):43–53, 1973
5. Beardsley, M. C. *Thinking Straight: Principles of Reasoning for Readers and Writers.* Prentice-Hall, Inc., Englewood Cliffs, N.J., 1975
6. Bernstein, T. M. *The Careful Writer: A Modern Guide to English Usage.* Atheneum, New York, 1973
7. Berthoff, A. E. *Forming, Thinking, Writing: the Composing Imagination.* Hayden Book Company, Inc., New York, 1978
8. Borko, H., and C. L. Bernier. *Abstracting Concepts and Methods.* Academic Press, New York, 1975
9. Borko, H., and S. Chatman. Criteria for acceptable abstracts: a survey of abstractors' instructions. *American Documentation* 14(2):149–160, 1963
10. Brusaw, C. T., G. J. Alred, and W. E. Oliu. *Handbook of Technical Writing.* St. Martin's Press, New York, 1976
11. Davis, C. H., and J. E. Rush. *Guide to Information Science.* Greenwood, Westport, Conn., 1979
12. Day, R. A. *How to Write and Publish a Scientific Paper.* ISI Press, Philadelphia, 1979
13. Griffith, B. C. Perspectives on cognition: human information processing (introduction). *Journal of the American Society for Information Science* 32(5):344–346, 1981
14. Griffith, B. C., and S. Crawford (eds.). Perspectives on cognition: human information processing. *Journal of the American Society for Information Science* 32(5):343–398, 1981
15. James, W. The energies of men. In *Essays on Faith and Morals,* selected by R. B. Perry, pp. 216–237. Longmans, Green, New York, 1947
16. Kain, J. F. A computer version of how a city works. *Fortune* 80(6):241–242, 1969
17. Klein, R., and M. D. Scheer. Addition of oxygen atoms to olefins at low temperature. IV. Rearrangements. *Journal of Physical Chemistry* 74(3):613–616, 1970
18. Kochen, M. Cognitive science. In J. Belzer, A. Holzman, and A. Kent (eds.), *Encyclopedia of Computer Science and Technology,* Volume 5. Marcel Dekker, Inc., New York, 1976 (cited in reference 28)
19. Koestler, A. The art of discovery and the discoveries of art. In *Bricks to Babel:*

144   *References*

a selection from 50 years of his writings, chosen and with new commentary by the author. Random House, New York, 1980

20. Lancaster, F. W., and S. Herner. Modular content analysis. *Proceedings of the American Documentation Institute*, 27th Annual Meeting, October 1964, Volume 1, pp. 403–405, 1964

21. Maizell, R. E., J. F. Smith, and T. E. R. Singer. *Abstracting Scientific and Technical Literature: an Introductory Guide and Text for Scientists, Abstractors, and Management*. Wiley-Interscience, New York, 1971

22. Mathis, B. A. *Techniques for the Evaluation and Improvement of Computer-Produced Abstracts*. OSU-CISRC-TR-79-15. The Computer and Information Science Research Center, The Ohio State University, Columbus, 1972.

23. Monsell, S. Representations, processes, memory mechanisms: the basic components of cognition. In B. C. Griffith and S. Crawford (eds.), Perspectives on cognition: human information processing. *Journal of the American Society for Information Science* 32(5):379–390, 1981

24. Pacifico, C. P. Thinking on thinking. Parts I–IV. *ChemTech*, February 1974, pp. 33–39; March 1974, pp. 147–152; June 1974, pp. 340–343; July 1974, pp. 406–411

25. Philler, T. A., R. K. Hersch, and H. V. Carlson (eds.) and B. H. Weil (consultant). *An Annotated Bibliography on Technical Writing, Editing, Graphics, and Publishing: 1950–1965*. Society of Technical Writers and Publishers, Inc., Washington, D.C., and Carnegie Library of Pittsburgh, Pittsburgh, Pa., 1966 (out of print)

26. Rowlett, R. Sidenotes for abstractors and section advisors. *CAS Report*, October 1980, p. 8

27. Simon, H. A. Information-processing models of cognition. In B. C. Griffith and S. Crawford (eds.), Perspectives on cognition: human information processing. *Journal of the American Society for Information Science* 32(5):364–377, 1981

28. Smith, L. C. Artificial Intelligence applications in information systems. In M. E. Williams (ed.), *Annual Review of Information Science and Technology*, Volume 15. Knowledge Industry Publications, Inc., White Plains, N.Y., 1980

29. Thomas, L. *The Medusa and the Snail; More Notes of a Biology Watcher*, pp. 6–9. Bantam Books, New York, 1974

30. Tichy, H. J. *Effective Writing: For Engineers, Managers, and Scientists*. John Wiley & Sons, Inc., New York, 1966

31. van Leunen, M. C. *A handbook for scholars*. Knopf, New York, 1978

32. Walker, D. E. The organization and use of information: contributions of information science, computational linguistics and artificial intelligence. In B. C. Griffith and S. Crawford (eds.), Perspectives on cognition: human information processing. *Journal of the American Society for Information Science* 32(5):347–363, 1981

33. Weil, B. H., I. Zarember, and H. Owen. Technical-abstracting fundamentals. I. Introduction. *Journal of Chemical Documentation* 3(1):86–89, 1963

34. Weil, B. H., I. Zarember, and H. Owen. Technical-abstracting fundamentals. II. Writing principles and practices. *Journal of Chemical Documentation* 3(2):125–132, 1963

35. Weil, B. H., I. Zarember, and H. Owen. Technical-abstracting fundamentals. III. Publishing abstracts in primary journals. *Journal of Chemical Documentation*, 3(2):132–136, 1963

36. White, H. D., and B. C. Griffith. Author cocitation: a literature measure of intellectual structure. *Journal of the American Society for Information Science* 32(3):163–171, 1981

37. Woodford, F. P. Sounder thinking through clearer writing. *Science* 156(3776):743–745, 1967

Index